To Jen

Where to Find Peace and Quiet

in

LONDON

— so ~et
~ n again

Love
Helen

COPYRIGHT

Where to Find Peace and Quiet in London

Copyright © 2017 by Elizabeth von Pier

Elizabeth von Pier
Cover design by Elizabeth von Pier
Photos by Elizabeth von Pier (exceptions are shown with credits)

First printing in August 2017

ISBN-13: 978-1548986285
ISBN-10: 1548986283

Disclaimer: Every effort was made to describe the information in this book accurately as of the publication date. Companies make periodic changes to their websites, practices, and policies, and so this information is subject to change. The author makes no guarantees regarding the information in this book. You should check directly with each company for the most up-to-date information regarding their practices, policies, pricing, etc.

Table of Contents

Forward, Credits and Acknowledgments v

Whitehall and Westminster
Banqueting House 8
Blewcoat School 10
Cloisters of Westminster Abbey 12

Piccadilly, St. James and Mayfair
Berkeley Square 14
Faraday Museum 16
Institute of Contemporary Arts 18
Mount Street Gardens 20
St. James Church 22
St. James Square 24
Spencer House 26
Spreads Cafe and Deli 28

Soho and Trafalgar Square
National Portrait Gallery 30
Photographers' Gallery 32
St. Martin-in-the-Fields 34

Covent Garden and the Strand
Art Gallery of the Courtauld Institute 36
London Transport Museum 38
The Queen's Chapel of the Savoy 40
St. Mary-le-Strand 42
St. Paul's Church 44
Victoria Embankment Gardens 46

Bloomsbury and Fitzrovia
Bloomsbury Square 48
British Library 50
Charles Dickens Museum 52
Fitzroy Square 54
Foundling Museum 56
Judd Street Open Space 58
Pollock's Toy Museum 60
Russell Square 62
St. Pancras Parish Church 64

Holborn and The Inns of Court
Lincoln's Inn and Lincoln's Inn Fields 66
Saint Andrew Holborn Church 68
Sir John Soane's Museum 70

TABLE OF CONTENTS - CONT'D

The City
Bank of England Museum	72
Guildhall Art Gallery	74
Garden of St. Michael's Cornhill	76
Courtyards of St. Paul's Cathedral	78
St. Stephen, Walbrook	80

Southwark and Bankside
Bankside Gallery	82
Millennium Courtyard of Southwark Cathedral	84

Chelsea and Battersea
Old English Garden in Battersea Park	86
Festival Pleasure Gardens in Battersea Park	88
Carlyle's House	90
Chelsea Physic Garden	92
Roper's Garden	94
Old Burial Ground, Royal Hospital of Chelsea	96
Saachi Gallery	98
Gardens of the Parish Church of St. Luke	100

Kensington and Holland Park
Design Museum	102
Japanese and Dutch Gardens in Holland Park	104
Italian Garden in Kensington Gardens	106
Kensington Roof Gardens	108
Leighton House Museum and Art Gallery	110
Margravine Cemetery	112
St. Mary Abbots Schoolyard and Alleyway	114
John Madejski Garden	116

Regent's Park and Marylebone
Little Venice and Regent's Canal	118
Wallace Collection	120
Waterside Cafe	122

Index	125

Forward, Credits and Acknowledgments

I love cities and in particular I love London. Westminster Abbey and Big Ben, Buckingham Palace and St. James Park, Holland Park and Notting Hill, afternoon tea and Georgian architecture, red telephone booths and double-decker buses, and yes, even the London Eye thrill me with all their British pomp and circumstance.

So, in the summers of 2016 and 2017, I set out to spend some time there and see it all. It was peak tourist season and crowds from all over the world were visiting the attractions, queuing up in lines as they maneuvered their way inch-by-inch to the entrances. The sights and attractions of London are mind-blowing and worth every bit of effort and time. But, at times, I found myself needing and seeking out places where I could, at least for a moment, enjoy some solitude, peace and quiet. There are many of these places and they are not that far from the crowds and horn-honking traffic. Here you can sit on a shady bench, listen to the birds or water flowing in a brook, sip a cup of tea, and rest and renew yourself.

This book describes the best quiet places I found. It includes small parks and squares, lovely old churches, small off-the-beaten-path museums and art galleries, hidden courtyards, and even cemeteries and tiny local eateries. It is organized around the major areas of the city and provides a full description of each restful retreat as well as practical information including closest Tube stop, nearby attractions, and hours. Sometimes, a few words about contiguous major landmarks are included. Many photographs are included to give the reader a sense of place.

All of the information in this book was taken from my personal impressions, materials obtained onsite, conversations with tour guides and docents, and official websites. The photographs are my own, with very few exceptions, and for those, credits are given with the photos.

I want to acknowledge and give special thanks to everyone who has supported me in this journey. In particular, I thank my sister and friend, Dr. Margaret Frieswyk, with whom I have spent many days traveling in foreign lands and who has encouraged me along the way. And special thanks to Corinne Anthony Becker who spent a month with me in Paris during my first year in retirement and who co-authored the daily journals that we sent to our friends and family back home, turning them into a novelette that had some of our readers anxiously awaiting the next installment about our French neighbor, Claire. That was the beginning of my new "career"—travel writing. And to all my friends and family who read my endless travel blogs, relived my journeys with me through my writings and photos, and encouraged me to do more, thank you.

Elizabeth von Pier
Hingham, Massachusetts

*Dedicated to
my family and friends,
with thanks for your help and support*

[8]

BANQUETING HOUSE

Location: Whitehall, across from the Horse Guards
Closest Underground Stations: Embankment, Westminster
Nearby Attractions: The London Eye, Horse Guards, Trafalgar Square, Big Ben
Open: 10am to 5pm daily, closed Sunday

THERE'S ONLY ONE ROOM TO SEE, BUT IT IS MAGNIFICENT—two stories high, white with gold trim, beautifully light-filled, and topped with a coffered ceiling covered with paintings by Rubens! This is the banqueting hall and it's all that remains of what once was the largest palace in Europe, extending from Trafalgar Square to Big Ben.

Start your visit with the ten-minute video of the history of the building, then pass the portrait of Charles I on the landing as you go up the stairs to the enormous room. The focal point is the ceiling. Other than this and exquisite architectural details, the room is mostly empty. For viewing comfort, you will find banquettes lining the walls, large "bean bags" on the floor, and three strategically placed tables with mirrors that reflect the ceiling. Claim one of the bean bags, lie down, listen to the tapes you received with your entry ticket, and enjoy the beauty up above.

The Rubens ceiling was commissioned by Charles I to glorify his father, James I, the man who built the house. It portrays the God-given rights of the kings. Three large allegorical paintings glorify James I and Charles I. The large oval in the ceiling's center shows James I in a red robe and gray beard being received into heaven as he rests his foot on a globe. Faith and Justice lead him to heaven and angels greet him blowing trumpets.

The building itself is of great architectural significance and a Registered Historic Palace. Designed by Inigo Jones for James I, it was completed in 1622 and was the first thoroughly classical building built in England. It is two-stories high with columns and pediments, and is situated on Whitehall right across from the Horse Guards.

In 1649, outside one of the windows of the first floor, King Charles was beheaded for treason following a short speech to the crowd gathered below. It is ironic that this ceiling was the last thing that Charles saw as he lifted, then lowered, his head to be beheaded. And we too rest our heads—on bean bags, not the executioner's scaffold—as we admire Rubens' ceiling up above.

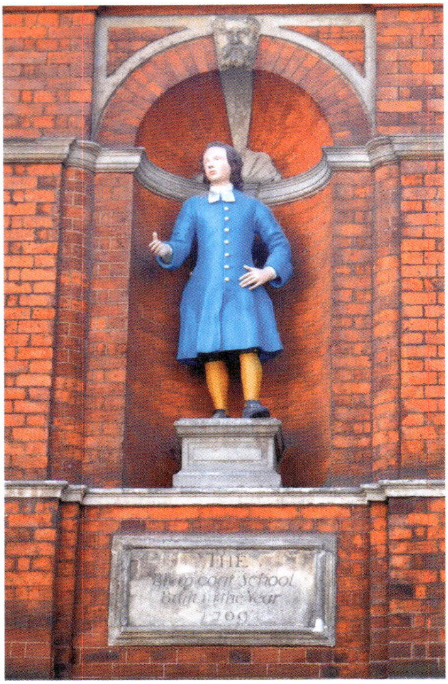
THE
School

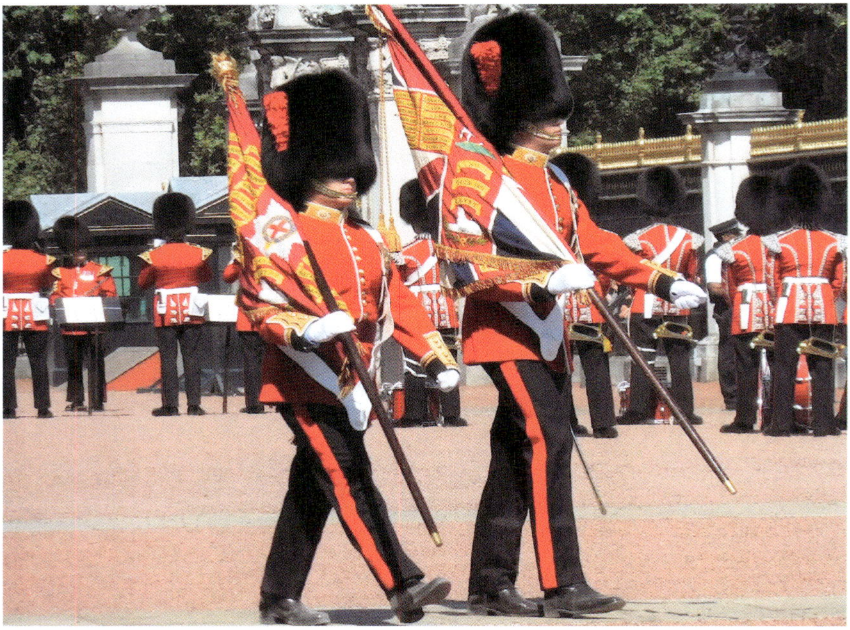

BLEWCOAT SCHOOL

Location: Caxton Street
Closest Underground Station: St. James Park
Nearby Attractions: Buckingham Palace, St. James Park
Open: Ian Stewart's shop hours are Tu, Wed, Fri, Sat 10am-6pm; Thurs 12:30-8:30pm

COME HERE FOR THE EXQUISITE LITTLE BUILDING more so than for the grounds. Built in 1709, the Blewcoat School was used as a charity school for the education of poor boys until 1926. Twenty boys were clothed and educated for free alongside a few fee-paying boys. For a period of time, girls were also admitted.

The school was purchased in 1954 by the National Trust and used as a gift shop and information center. Then in 2013 fashion designer Ian Stewart was granted permission to refurbish the space to showcase his exclusive wedding and ball gown collections.

It is a small cube of a building made of red and yellow brick with stone dressings and recessed niches sheltering statues of blewcoats. Along the side of the building are raised beds with tall shady trees and some wide staircases. This is a good place to sit and enjoy the beauty of the building. You can also go inside to admire the Baroque architecture and the single pine-paneled room with its light, airy coved ceiling. The chandelier comes from Bruerne Abbey in Oxfordshire.

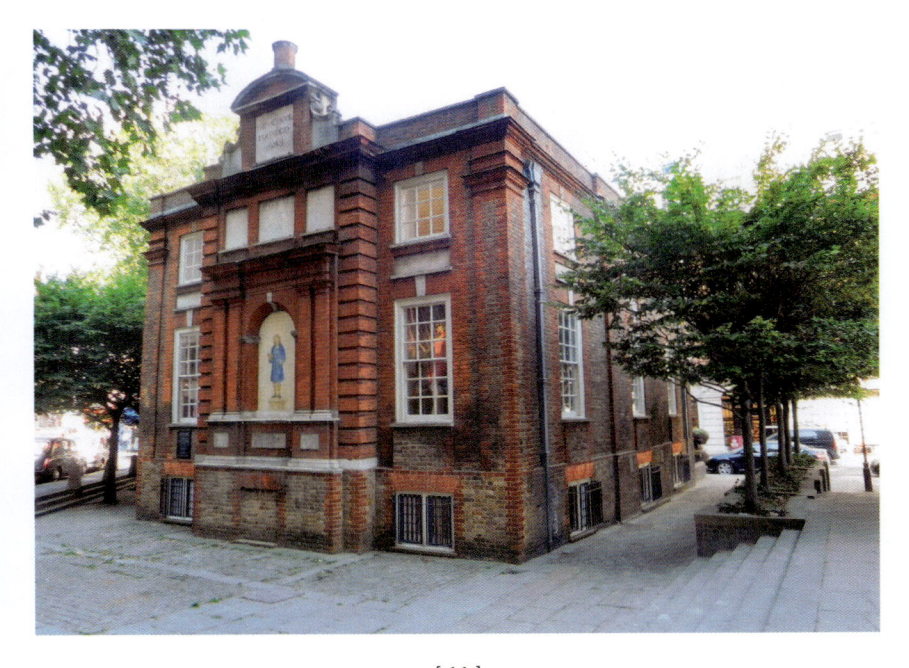

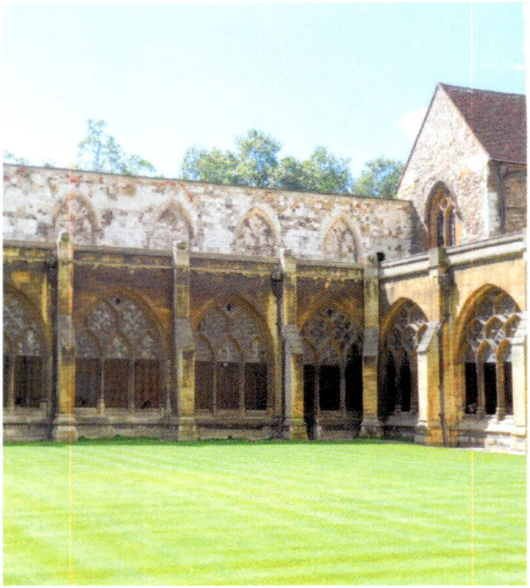

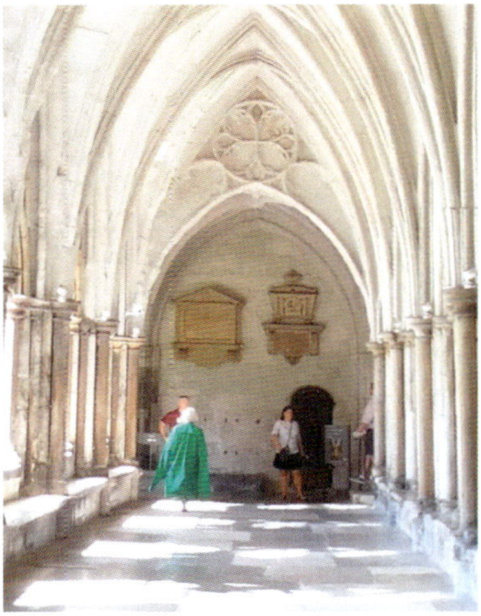

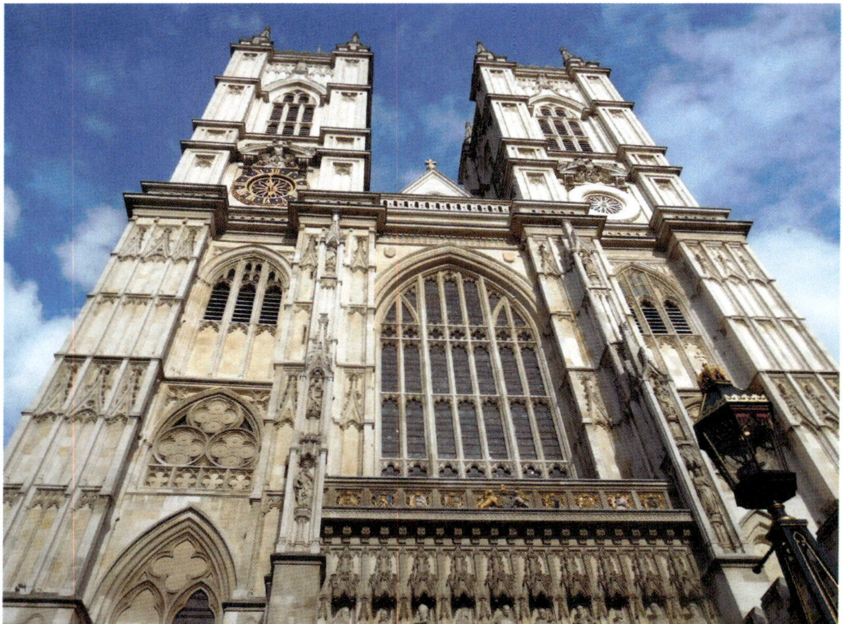

Cloisters of Westminster Abbey

Location: Westminster Abbey
Closest Underground Stations: Westminster, St. James Park
Nearby Attractions: Westminster Abbey, Houses of Parliament, Big Ben
Hours: 9am-6pm daily

WESTMINSTER ABBEY IS USUALLY OVERFLOWING WITH TOURISTS and might seem like an unlikely place to find some peace and quiet. However, situated next to the nave and connecting the Abbey church with the other buildings are the cloisters, a good place to escape the masses of people inside.

The cloisters were built during the 13th and 14th centuries and were where the Benedictine monks were required to spend much of their time in seclusion. I imagine them sitting there in the sun, sheltered from the wind, meditating or reading their bibles. Still today, the cloisters offer a sense of serenity. There are lovely views across a grassy courtyard towards Victoria Tower, and memorials and plaques honoring the dead line the walls and the floors on which you walk. This is where high-ranking monks were buried; their juniors were interred in the garth.

The Abbey itself dates from the 13th century and is world-renowned as the burial site for British monarchs and the traditional place where coronations and royal weddings are celebrated. Inside the mammoth building is the Grave of the Unknown Warrior killed during the First World War and the only one in the Abbey on which it is forbidden to walk. The Coronation Chair is there too, constructed in 1301 and used at every coronation since 1308. And you'll find the graves of Isaac Newton (1727), Charles Darwin (1882), and Geoffrey Chaucer (1400) who is buried here along with other poets and writers in what has come to be known as Poets' Corner. The funeral of Diana, Princess of Wales, was held here, and the wedding of Prince William, Duke of Cambridge, and Catherine Middleton took place at Westminster Abbey in 2011.

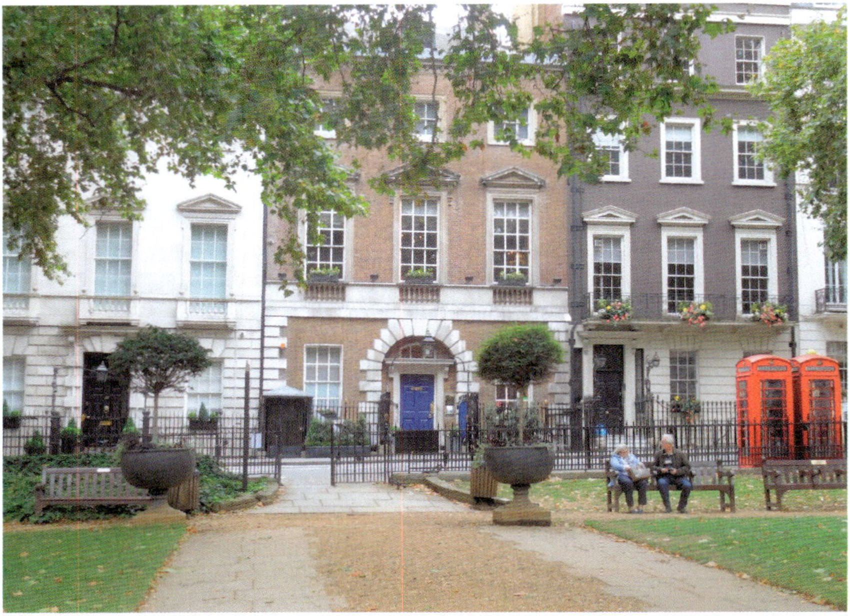

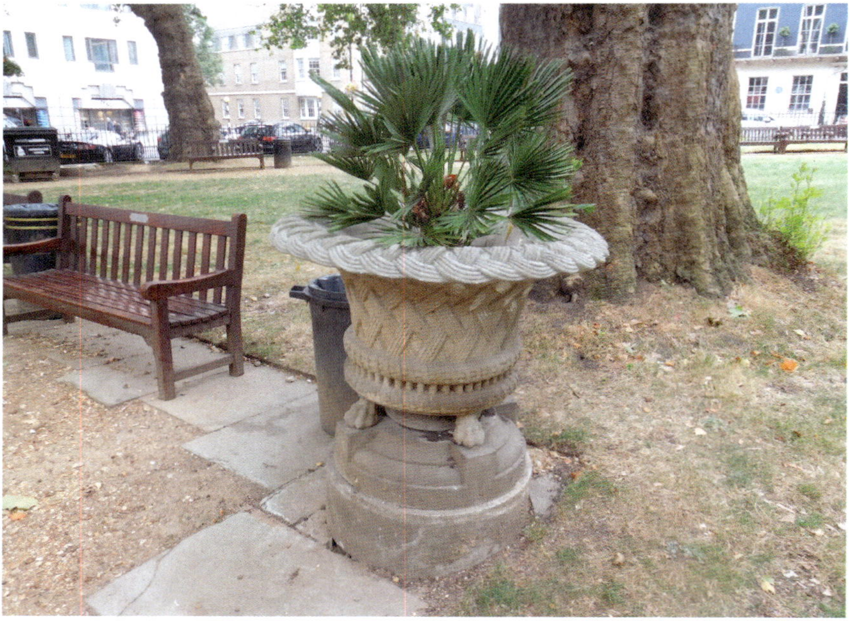

Berkeley Square

Location: Off Bruton Street in Mayfair
Closest Underground Station: Green Park
Nearby Attractions: Hyde Park, Green Park, Bond Street and Regent Street shopping

BERKELEY SQUARE HAS ALWAYS BEEN A FASHIONABLE ADDRESS IN MAYFAIR in the West End of London. Surrounding the square are beautiful 18th century buildings which today house wealth management companies and financial advisers as well as cafes, posh hotels, art galleries and luxury car showrooms. In 1745 when the square was laid out, you would have found a carpenter, wax chandler, woolen draper, undertaker, distiller, hosier, tailor and apothecary.

Part of the square's history is a haunted townhouse at 50 Berkeley Square. In the late 1800's, its occupant, a Mr. Myers, became a recluse after his fiancée ditched him, and he moved to a tiny room on the top floor, coming out only at night to roam the hallways. Strange things started happening—in fact, two servants died from fright after cleaning there. Currently the townhouse is used for offices. There are still complaints of strange occurrences although it looks perfectly normal to the casual passerby.

The square is home to the finest and oldest of London's plane trees, many of them over 250 years old, and there are plenty of benches where you can rest your tired feet in some aristocratic surroundings. There is only one statue in the square, a nymph which was erected in 1858 at the entrance. She is made of fine Carrera marble and is semi-draped and carrying a vase. At the time, it was commonly felt that she was superior to Venus de Milo.

[16]

FARADAY MUSEUM

Location: In the Royal Institution building at 21 Albermarle Street, St. James
Closest Underground Station: Green Park
Nearby Attractions: Green Park, Piccadilly Circus, St. James Church, Bond Street shopping
Hours: 9am to 6pm Mon.-Fri., closed Sat.-Sun.
Admission: Free

MICHAEL FARADAY (1791-1867) WAS A PIONEER IN THE USES OF ELECTRICITY and his discoveries, made in the basement of the Royal Institution at 21 Albermarle Street in London, shaped the modern world.

Faraday came from humble beginnings and went on to become one of the most renowned scientists in history. He invented the electric motor and is generally credited with the discovery in 1831 of electromagnetic induction, the principle behind the transfer of an electromotive force across a conductor exposed to changes in magnetic fields.

You will find the small but fascinating Faraday Museum on the lower ground floor of the RI building tucked in with other scientific displays in well-lit glass cases. The highlight of the exhibition is Faraday's magnetic laboratory as it was in the 1850s (and in its original spot) opposite a current state-of-the-art version. You can see his giant electro-magnet, at the time the most powerful magnet in the country, the original electrostatic generator which he made while still a bookbinder's apprentice, and various woodworking tools and scientific equipment he invented.

The RI building has several floors which are used for other scientific displays, a scientific library, a lecture hall and an excellent cafe.

[18]

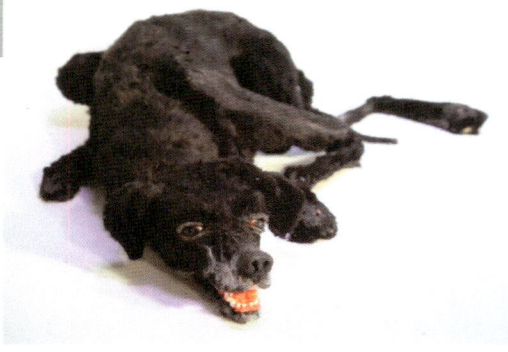

Institute of Contemporary Arts

Location: The Mall
Closest Underground Stations: Piccadilly Circus, Charing Cross
Nearby Attractions: National Gallery, Trafalgar Square, St. James Park
Open: 11am to 6pm Tues.-Sun., closed Mon.

HOUSED IN JOHN NASH'S CLASSICAL CARLTON HOUSE TERRACE (1833), the ICA has been an avant-garde arts and entertainment venue since 1947. It's been in this location since 1968 and consists of three art galleries, a movie theater, an auditorium, a performance theater for plays, dance and music, a reading room, a gift shop, and a bar and cafe.

The art galleries showcase works of artists using various media within the genre of "radical modern". In the summer of 2017, one gallery was devoted to a single work of art, a floor made from reclaimed boards and joists. Another had an interesting collection of black and white woodcuts with subjects ranging from bureaucracy to the objectification of women to rituals and practices that defined urban life in an anonymous metropolis in the early 1920s. And a third consisted of short films of a dog—barking ferociously, wagging his tail, and walking. Indeed, the exhibits at the ICA are avant-garde and may not be for everyone.

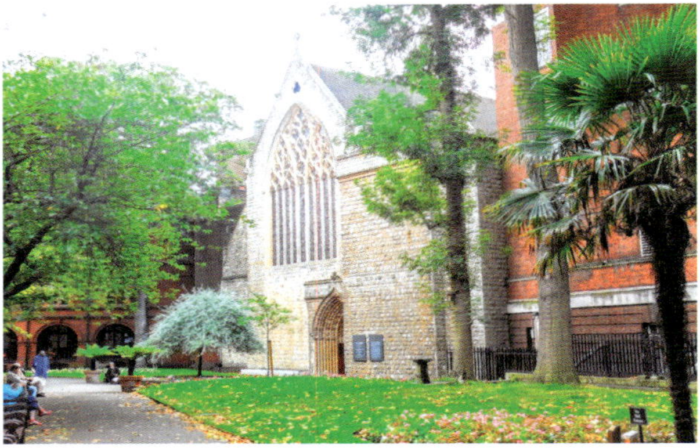

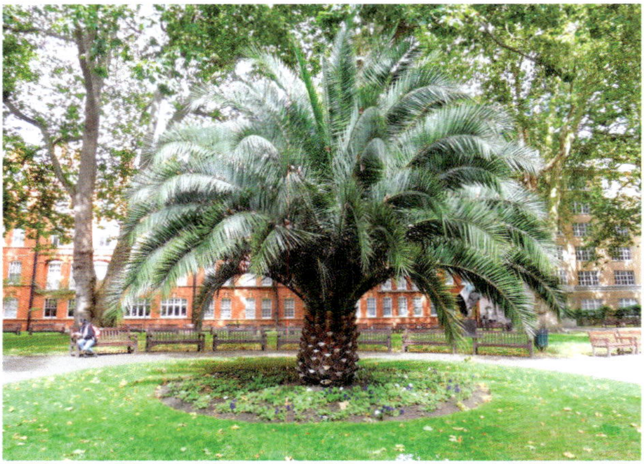

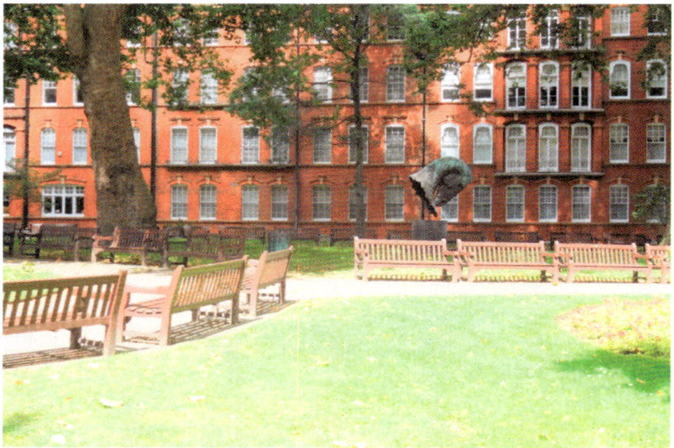

MOUNT STREET GARDENS

Location: Mayfair, two entrances on Mount Street and one on South Audley Street
Closest Underground Stations: Green Park, Bond Street
Nearby Attractions: Green Park, Bond Street and Regent Street shopping, Faraday Museum

IT'S WORTH LOOKING FOR THIS SECRET GEM hidden behind houses and mansion blocks in a quiet residential area of upscale Mayfair. The gardens were created in 1889 on the site of a former burial ground. They back onto the neo-Gothic Church of the Immaculate Conception which was completed forty years earlier. It is quiet and small and there are plenty of benches that have been donated in memory of those who have loved and enjoyed the park.

The foliage consists of majestic London plane trees, formal lawns and ornamental beds. A Canary Island palm thrives here because the climate is suitable—not only is the park sheltered but also because central London is slightly warmer than elsewhere around the city. Robins, great tits, magpies and blackbirds are frequent visitors. Also within the park is a bronze drinking fountain of a rearing horse, a bird bath and a bird identification panel. This is a lush little oasis that you should not miss.

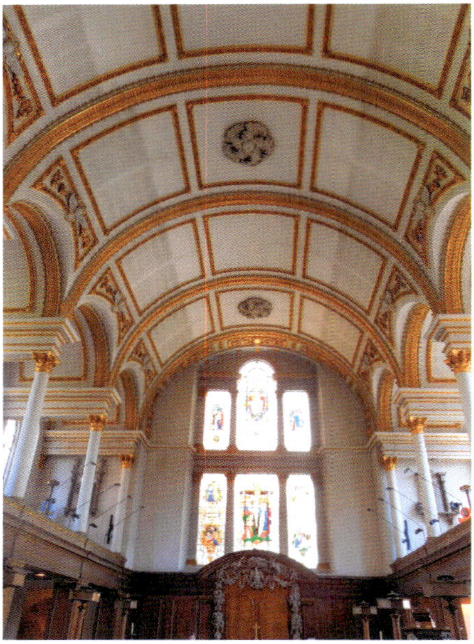

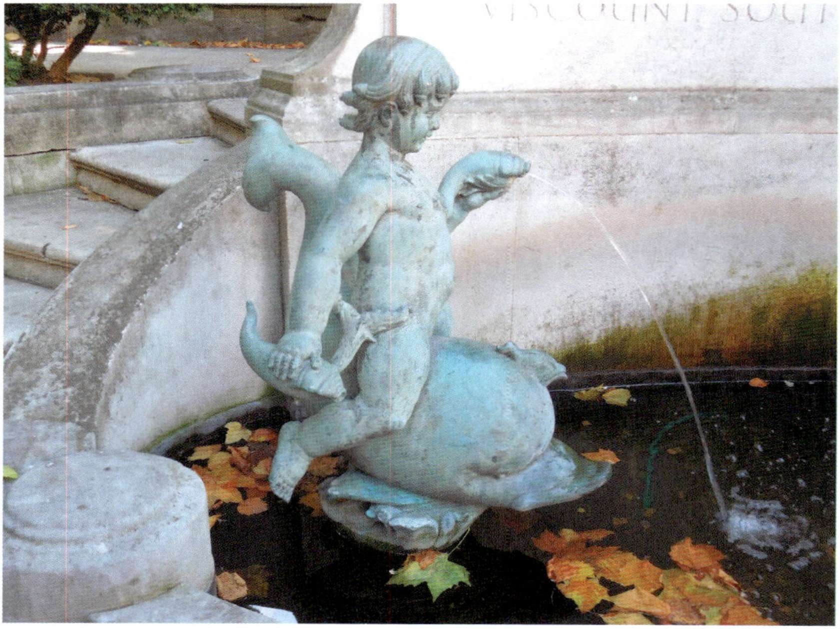
VISCOUNT

St. James Church

Location: 197 Piccadilly, in the West End
Closest Underground Station: Piccadilly Circus
Nearby Attractions: Piccadilly Circus, National Gallery, Trafalgar Square

Rather than the church itself, you first notice the Piccadilly Market that is held Monday through Saturday on the square out front. Booths offering everything from burgers, quinoa salad and cookies to oil paintings, Venetian glass and collectibles are set up under canopies and trees. It's a busy area full of office workers and locals, and church bells ring every half hour.

Off to the right and up a set of stairs is the Southwood Garden flanked by large statues of fish spurting jets of water into the pool below. Opened in 1946 by Queen Mary, it is a place for quiet contemplation and used by the community for lunch breaks. One side has been set up for a drop-in counseling service, an outreach ministry supported by the church.

St. James is a Church of England parish and has an active, open and affirming congregation welcoming people of many different faiths and beliefs. It even supports a vagabonds group of spiritual enquirers who meet in an alehouse because they prefer the alehouse to the church.

The building is one of many designed by architect Christopher Wren and considered to be among his finest endeavors. It is handsome made of red brick with stone dressings. Dedicated in 1684, St. James has a Grade I heritage designation.

Have lunch in the courtyard, then go into the church at 1:10 pm for a free recital held every Monday, Wednesday and Friday, a perfect respite from the noise and activity outside.

[24]

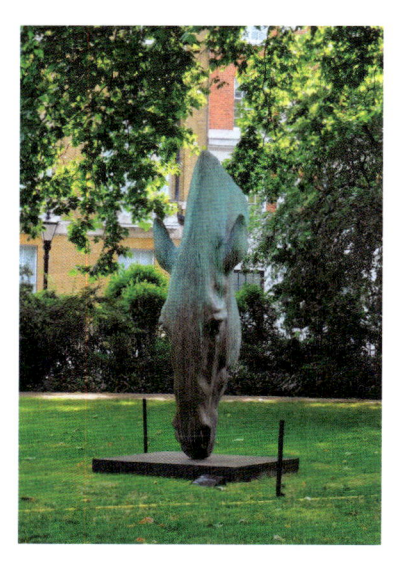

St. James Square

Location: Close to Pall Mall in St. James, Westminster
Closest Underground Stations: Green Park, Piccadilly Circus
Nearby Attractions: Piccadilly Circus, Trafalgar Square, National Gallery
Open to the public on weekdays only, to 4:30 pm

I WAS DELIGHTED WHEN I CAME UPON THIS STATELY SQUARE in the exclusive West end. It's set one block in from busy Pall Mall and off the beaten path so I took a detour from my route and followed the marker to a lovely spot that was almost empty except for a few birds and nannies with baby carriages.

John Nash designed the square and it is maintained and cared for by the St James's Square Trust. Stately Georgian and neo-Georgian buildings line the streets; in fact, seventeen out of twenty-five are "listed" as properties of special importance. They were built as "dwellings for Noblemen and other persons of quality" whose business required them to be near St. James's Palace, but today they are private clubs and headquarters for some well known companies. At one time, number 4 was home to Nancy Astor, the first woman to sit in Parliament, and three prime ministers lived at number 10.

The square was laid out in the 1670s and in the gardens in the center, set on a pedestal, is an equestrian statue of William III that's been here since 1808. There are benches carefully placed under shade trees and spaced well apart so that you can have some privacy. A special *Sculpture in the Square* exhibit by Christie's auction house was on display and included some unique modern and traditional art that provided the perfect counterpoint to the historic square.

Pick up some take-out from St. James Caffe around the corner at 41 Pall Mall and enjoy it sitting on a bench in this lovely space.

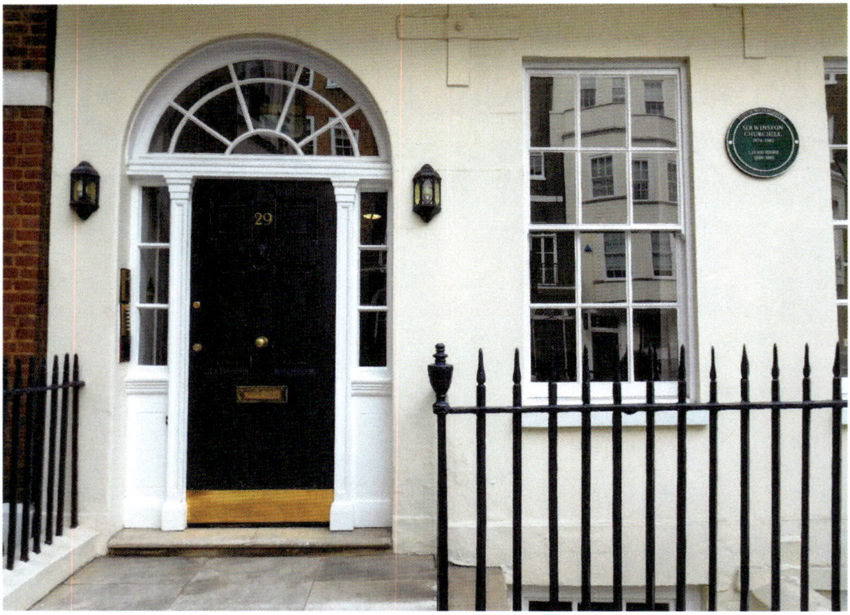
29
SIR WINSTON
CHURCHILL

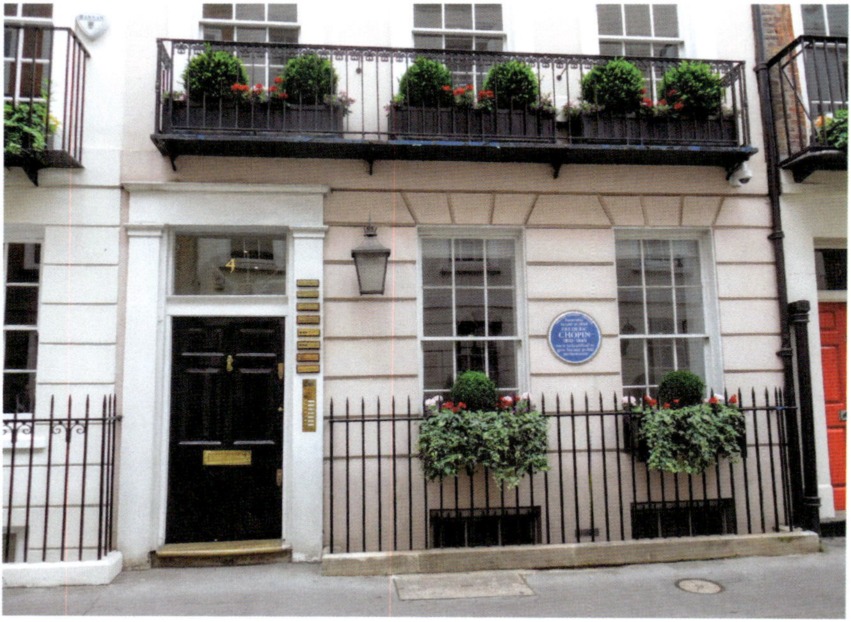
4
CHOPIN

Spencer House

Location: 27 St. James Place, Westminster
Closest Underground Station: Green Park
Nearby Attractions: Buckingham Palace, Green Park, St. James Park
Hours: 10:30am to 5:45pm Sunday

THIS ANCESTRY HOME OF THE FAMILY OF THE LATE DIANA, Princess of Wales, is an elegant 18th century townhouse built in 1766 for John, first Earl of Spencer. It is an ambitious and splendid palace that uses designs from ancient Rome including a Palladian facade and a pediment adorned with classical statues. The house has been restored to its original splendor and today it is the city's only great 18th century house to survive intact.

Inside on the first floor is the Painted Room, one of the State rooms, magnificently gilded and beautifully decorated. On the second floor is the lavish and exquisite Palm Room, painted pale green and decorated with columns, niches, statuary, and gilded carvings that resemble gold palm trees, the symbol of marital fertility. Look closely and you will find smaller palm trees adorning the mirrors and chandeliers.

The Spencers no longer live here; it is mainly rented out for functions. They also sold off most of the furniture so you get to see only a sampling. But the structure and décor nevertheless are in keeping with the times and beautiful to behold.

This area was home to other notables besides the Spencers. As you walk up St. James Place toward the palace, you will notice that Chopin lived at number 4, and Winston Churchill at number 29.

It is mandatory to book a one-hour tour in order to see this house. The tour is preceded by a ten-minute video.

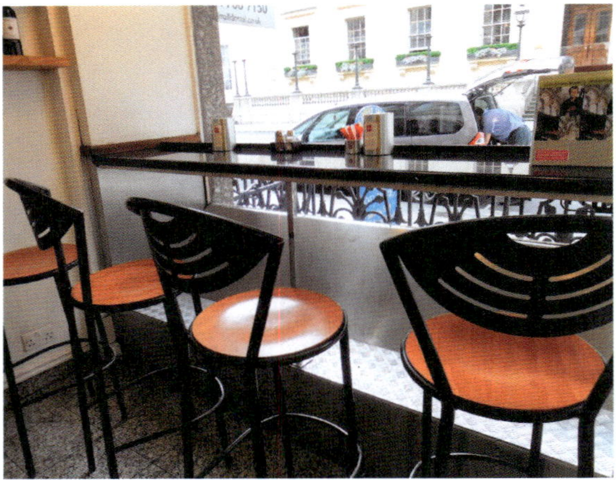

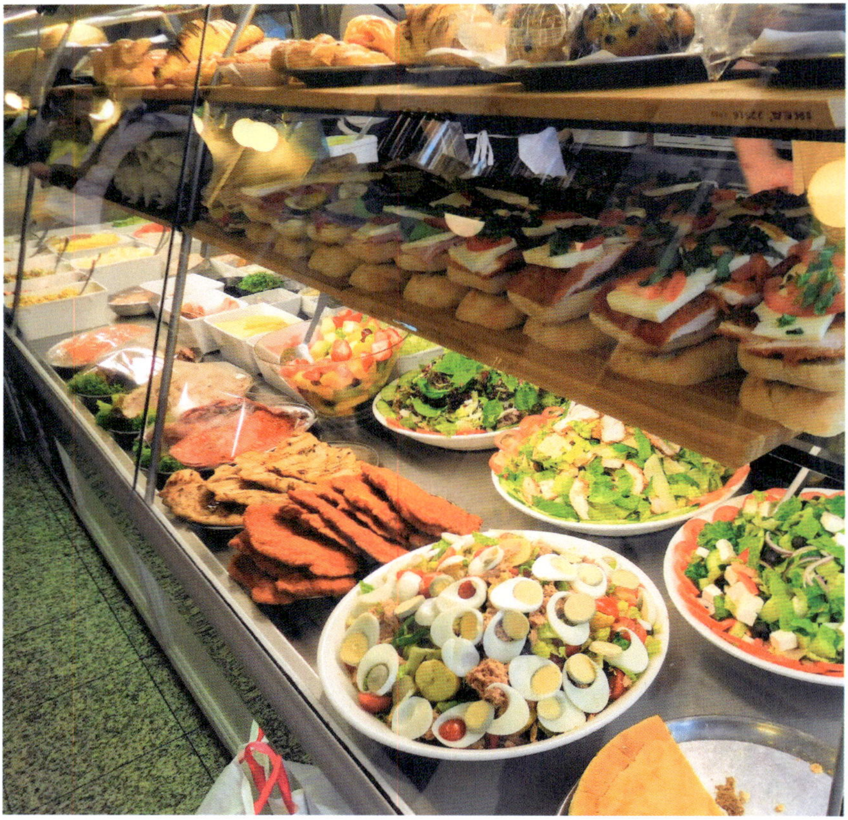

SPREADS CAFE AND DELI

Location: 15A Pall Mall
Closest Underground Stations: Piccadilly, Charing Cross
Nearby Attractions: National Gallery, Trafalgar Square, Piccadilly Square
Hours: 7am to 5pm, closed Sunday

IF YOU'RE LOOKING FOR A SMALL LOCALLY-OWNED AND OPERATED RESTAURANT with a local following and a mouthwatering assortment of pastries, fruits, salads, pasta dishes, and sandwiches, Spreads Cafe and Deli is for you. Its location is ideal, just steps from the National Gallery, Trafalgar Square and Piccadilly Square.

Spreads will prepare your food to order and accommodate special requests. And it also has a full breakfast menu including freshly made omelets and egg dishes, and delicious coffees made from beans imported from Italy.

I walked in, ordered from the tempting displays under glass at the counter, and chose a seat looking out onto the street. As I sat there, taxi drivers and local business people came in, briefcases in hand, and took tables in the back of the tiny restaurant. My order was a tomato, burrata, basil and prosciutto baguette, and there was no problem serving me typical lunch food at breakfast time. As I savored my meal, I observed a steady stream of people ordering takeout coffees, pastries and croissants, and one of the four employees was preparing a platter of fresh fruit for delivery to a local office.

Spreads is London-based and offers cafe and catering services from two locations—this one in the upscale West End and another just east of London in the Lakeside Shopping Center at Brompton Walk in Thurrock. They have been in business for over 30 years.

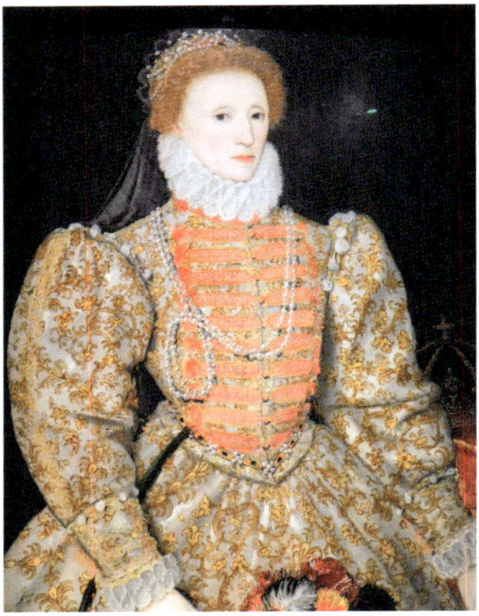
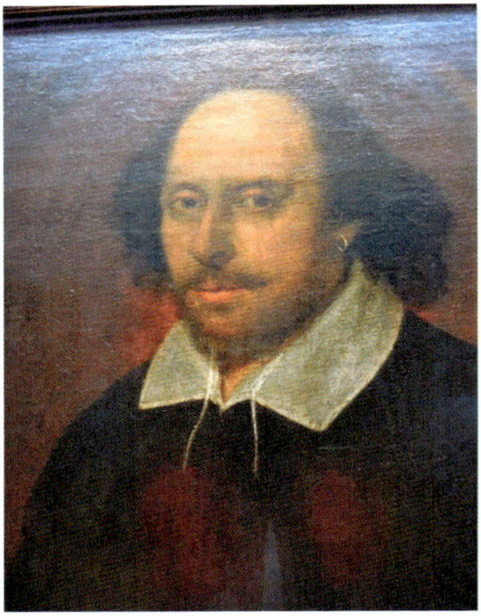
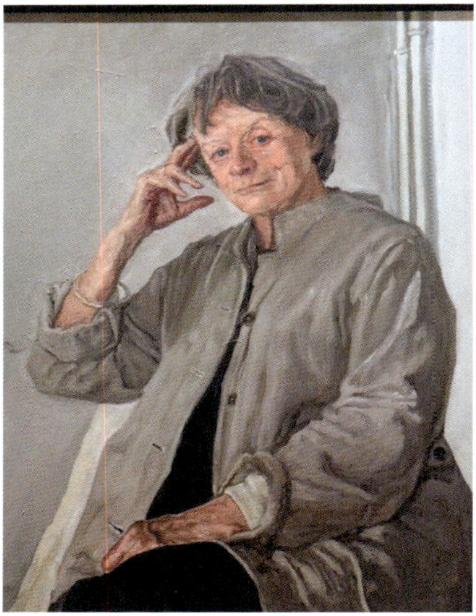
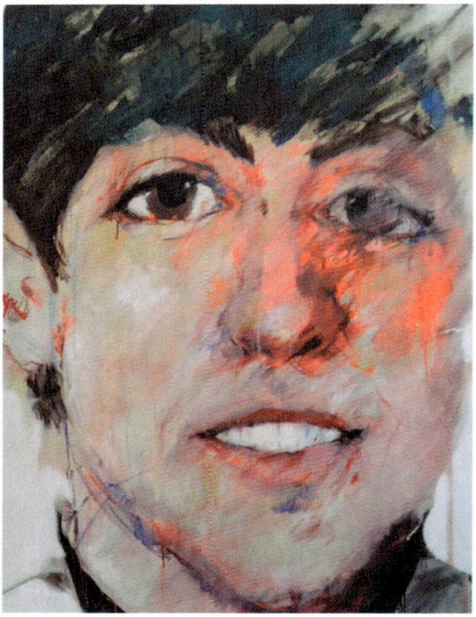

National Portrait Gallery

Location: 2 St. Martin's Place
Closest Underground Stations: Charing Cross, Leicester Square
Nearby Attractions: National Gallery, Trafalgar Square, Piccadilly Circus
Open: Daily 10am-6pm, Thursday and Friday until 9pm
Admission: Free

I CAME HERE FOR HIGH TEA AND DISCOVERED A FASCINATING MUSEUM that traces 500 years of British history through portraits of famous (and infamous) men and women. The gallery was founded in 1856 and contains 160,000 portraits of royalty, writers, politicians, scientists, artists, actors and musicians from all periods since the 14th century.

Some of the most notable works are located in the new Ondaatje Wing on the second floor. Shakespeare by Taylor is in Room 4; three portraits of Elizabeth I, including the most famous one by Ditchley, are in Room 3; Isaac Newton is in Room 8; and George Washington is in Room 14. The most famous portrait of Henry VIII is a Holbein miniature in Room 1 in the Tudor Gallery. Portraits from the 1960s to 1990s including the current royal family are on the balcony in this wing. You will also find a few ghoulish and creepy pieces.

The Portrait Restaurant on the top floor has gorgeous views overlooking Trafalgar Square. In addition to light breakfasts, lunches, and Sunday Roasts, they also serve afternoon tea starting at 3:30. You get a tiered plate of savories and sweets, plus their own tea.

The gallery has halls and education studios where they offer lunchtime lectures, weekend workshops, films and talks, and there is a Portrait Choir that performs choral works inspired by the collections.

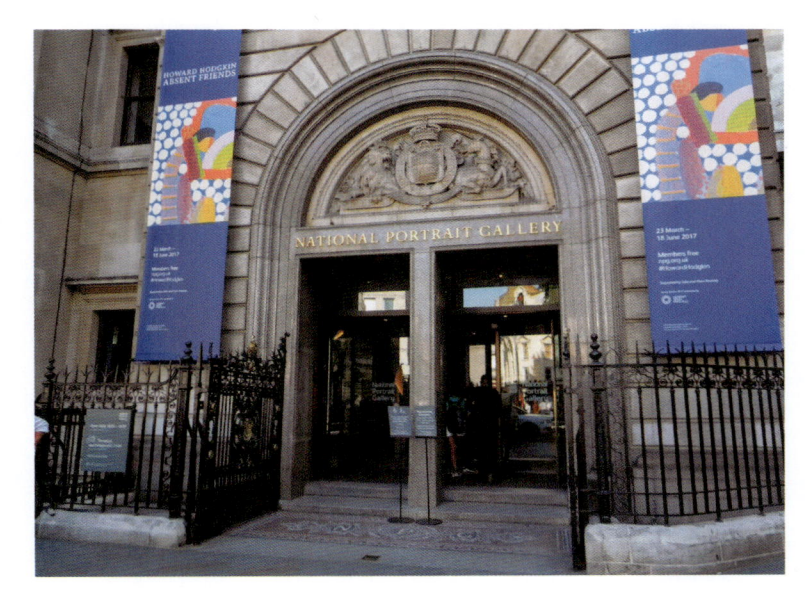

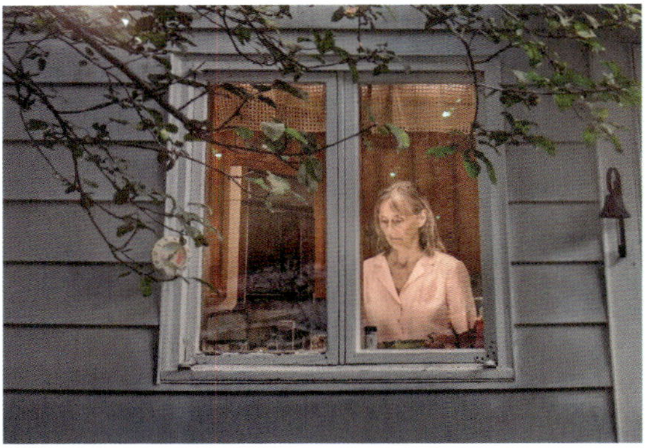

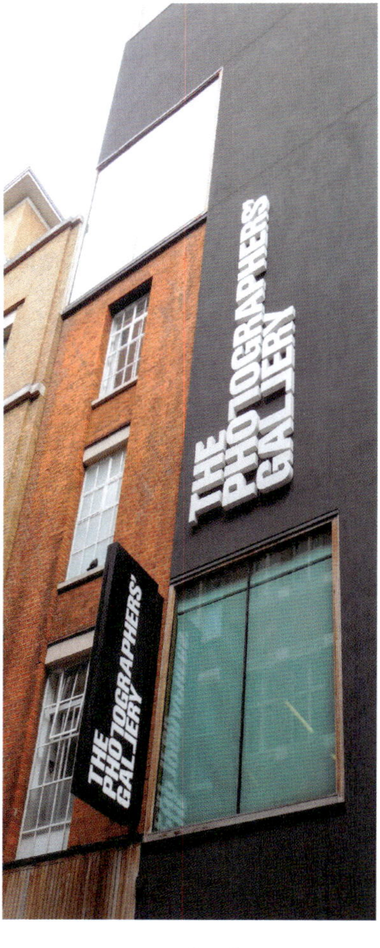
THE PHOTOGRAPHERS' GALLERY
THE PHOTOGRAPHERS' GALLERY

Photographers' Gallery

Location: 16-18 Ramillies Street
Closest Underground Station: Oxford Circus
Nearby Attractions: Oxford Street shopping, Langham (historic) Hotel
Hours: 10am-6pm Mon.-Sat., 11am-6pm Sun.
Admission: Free before noon

ESTABLISHED IN 1971, the Photographers' Gallery is the UK's leading center for the presentation and exploration of all forms of photography and a resource for the international photographic community. The Gallery supports the works of both new talent and renowned photographers, and it is not uncommon for a newcomer to gain worldwide status after exhibiting here. There also is an excellent program of events and educational talks, and a cafe/bar on the ground floor where you can get a bite to eat and escape the crowds on nearby Oxford Street.

When I was there in the summer of 2017, the gallery had devoted all three of its floors to the work of American artist Gregory Crewdson. Crewdson's exhibit, entitled *Cathedral of the Pines*, explored often deeply disturbing "tensions between human connection and separation, intimacy and isolation", as portrayed by people posing in the small hill town of Becket, Massachusetts.

JANE MARY LYLE
Grand Mother to the Above
JOHN THOMAS
Monument

St. Martin-in-the-Fields

Location: Trafalgar Square
Closest Underground Station: Charing Cross
Nearby Attractions: National Gallery, Trafalgar Square, National Portrait Gallery

THIS CHURCH IS HOME TO THE ACADEMY OF ST. MARTIN-IN-THE-FIELDS, a world renowned chamber orchestra, and three high-quality choral groups. You may be lucky to catch one of their free lunchtime concerts or a rehearsal for an evening event. Mid-afternoon on a Saturday in the summer, I just happened in and listened to inspiring music coming from a group of talented artists practicing for the Vivaldi concert that night.

There has been a church in this spot since medieval times. In 1726 James Gibbs designed the current church building in a simple neoclassical style that has been copied throughout North America. The window behind the altar is new and displays a stylized cross that is unique (and controversial) among parishioners and visitors.

St. Martin's uses the medium of music to increase cultural awareness and advance its commitment to social justice, humanitarianism and international issues. The acoustics in the church are superb, and Handel and Mozart performed here. In 1990, a new pipe organ was acquired that is considered to be one of the finest in London.

Downstairs in the crypt are some old tombs, a gift shop and bookstore, a unique restaurant, and a brass rubbing center where you can practice the Victorian craft. The entrance to the crypt is in a glass elevator/stairwell enclosure to the left of the church building.

This church has it all, providing fuel for the mind, the body and the soul.

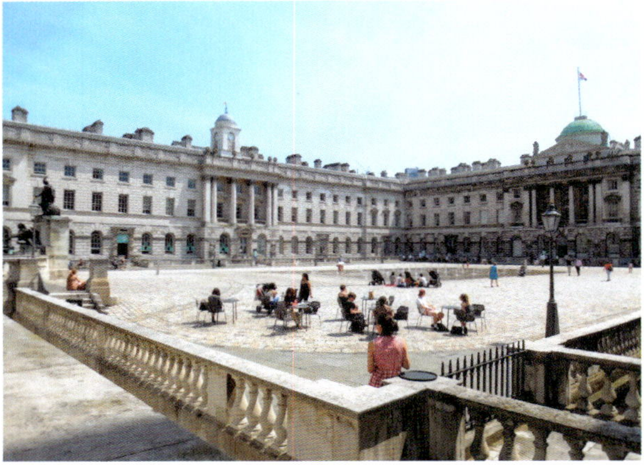

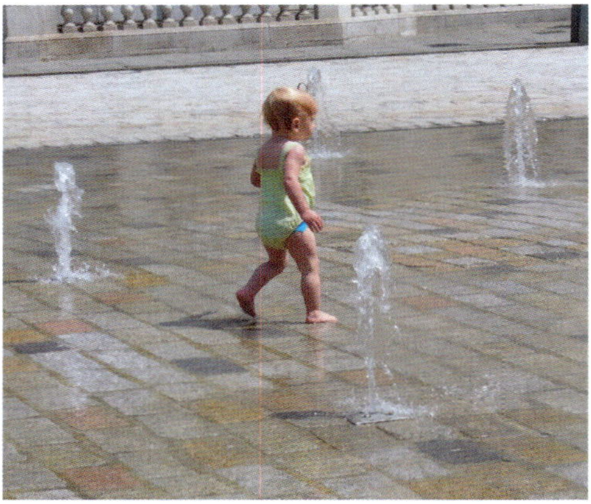

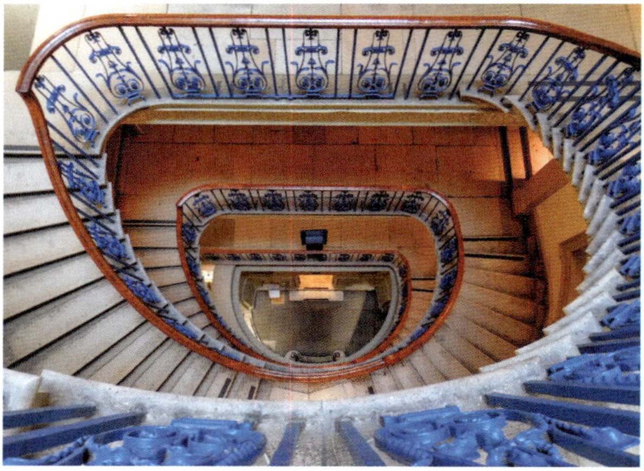

ART GALLERY OF THE COURTAULD INSTITUTE

Location: Inside Somerset House; closest entrance on the Strand
Closest Underground Station: Temple
Nearby Attractions: The Queen's Walk, London Transport Museum, Savoy Chapel
Hours: 10am-6pm daily

IF YOU LIKE IMPRESSIONIST ART IN AN ELEGANT SETTING, you should not miss this one. Works by Manet, Monet, Degas, Cezanne, Pissaro, Van Gogh and others are housed inside the Somerset House, a grand 18th century neoclassical townhouse that is a major venue for the arts and culture. The collection also includes medieval European paintings and altarpieces and spans the history of Western art, but the impressionists and post-impressionists are particularly well represented. The most famous works are Manet's *Bar at the Follies-Bergere*, Van Gogh's *Self Portrait with a Bandaged Ear*, and Monet's *Autumn Effect at Argenteuil*.

The museum is named after Samuel Courtauld (1876-1947) who was a wealthy textile magnate and philanthropist. In 1931, he donated his art collection to the museum, and other patrons added to it. Today, it contains one of the finest collections of impressionist and post-impressionist paintings in the world. The Gallery is part of an art institute and a place used for teaching, so clear and detailed descriptions are included with each piece of art. This makes for a very thorough educational experience if you can spend the time.

Be sure to enjoy the playful fountains in the courtyard of Somerset House, a good place to cool off on a hot day in London. Not far away, between the Strand and the Thames, you will find several fine eateries, some ideally situated on the terrace overlooking the river. The Courtauld also has its own outdoor cafe with a nice selection of light meals to be enjoyed throughout the day.

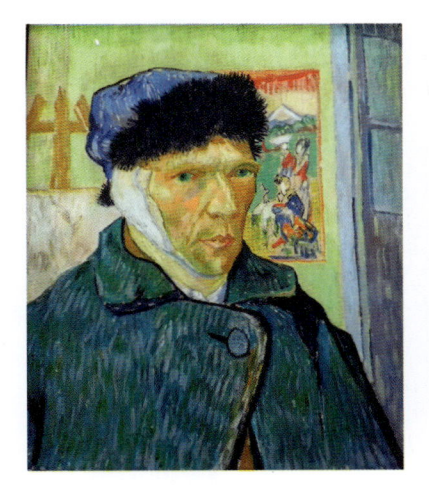

[38]

LONDON TRANSPORT MUSEUM

Location: Covent Garden Piazza
Closest Underground Station: Covent Garden
Nearby Attractions: The Strand, Somerset House, Savoy Chapel, St. Paul's Church
Hours: 10am-6pm Sat.-Thurs., 11am-6pm Fri.

𝔥OUSED IN A PICTURESQUE OLD VICTORIAN FLOWER MARKET, the London Transport Museum covers the history of public transportation from 1800 when horse-drawn carriages were used, to the growth of the suburbs and the steam underground, to modes not yet developed. Old trolleys, taxis, buses and the Tube are on display, and you are allowed to board many of the old vehicles. You will also find posters, commercial art, photographs, and interactive exhibits including a simulation of driving the Tube train.

It is fitting that such a fine museum be located here right in the heart of London, for the city's growth was made possible by its system of public transportation. In fact, the idea of public buses originated in London—people could board a vehicle without a reservation and travel from one part of the city to another on a set route and at a reasonable cost. This was a novel idea at the time, but how we take it for granted today.

To visit the museum chronologically, start on the top floor and work your way down. In order to qualify as one of the quieter places to visit in London, do not come on weekends when it is filled with children and their parents clamoring to put themselves in the driver's seat of a London bus or train.

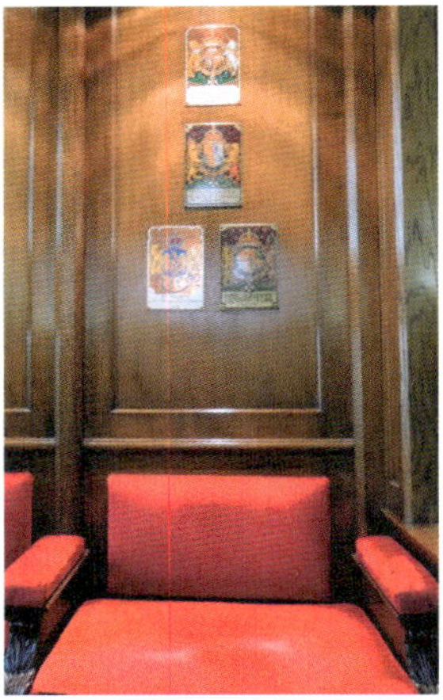

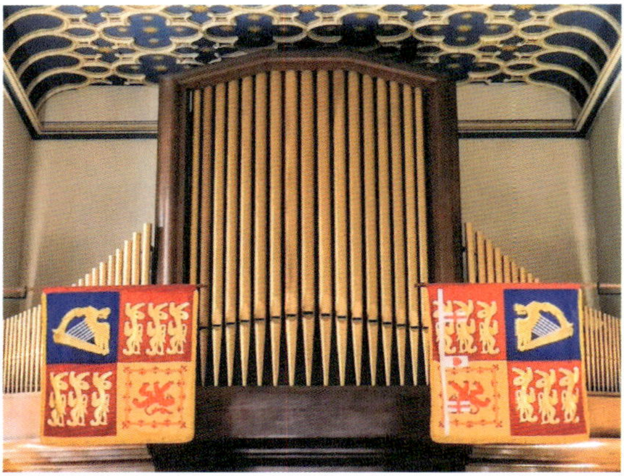

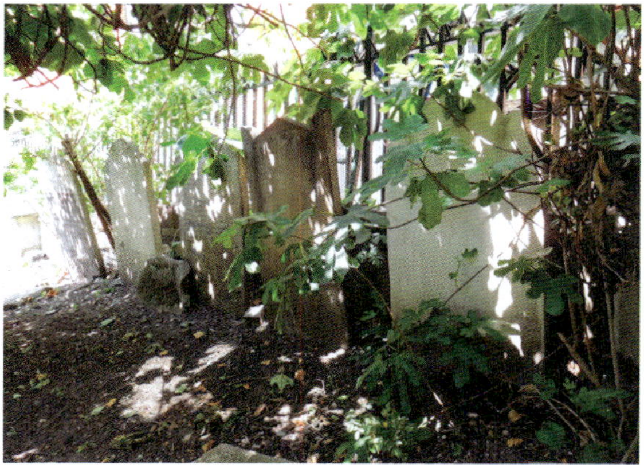

The Queen's Chapel of the Savoy

Location: Savoy Hill off Savoy Place
Closest Underground Stations: Charing Cross, Embankment
Nearby Attractions: Victoria Embankment Gardens, Somerset House
Hours: 9am-4pm Mon.-Thurs., 9am-1pm Sun., closed Fri.-Sat. and Aug.-Sept.

It MAY BE A LITTLE HARD TO FIND THE ENTRANCE TO THIS GEM but make the effort and you will be glad that you did. Look for Savoy Place off the Strand, pass the church graveyard (now a pleasant courtyard), then go down the hill and take a right on Savoy Hill.

The Queen's Chapel was built in 1515 as part of a charitable foundation to provide a night's lodging for one hundred "pour and nedie" men under the terms of the will of King Henry VII. It was a large complex that included a hospital, dormitory and three chapels. Most was demolished in the early nineteenth century except for the Chapel of St. John the Baptist, now known as the Queen's Chapel of the Savoy.

It is called the "Queen's Chapel" because it is Crown property and has for centuries been under the jurisdiction of the reigning monarch rather than a bishop. Her Majesty does not usually worship here but there is plenty of evidence of royalty, including a set of banners that hangs near the entrance and a large red chair that displays armorial plates of the Queen's coat of arms.

Notice the font made in 1865 of caen stone with a canopy of carved oak at the west end of the sanctuary. The stained glass window that depicts a procession of musicians is dedicated to the memory of Richard D'Oyly Carte who was married in the chapel in 1888.

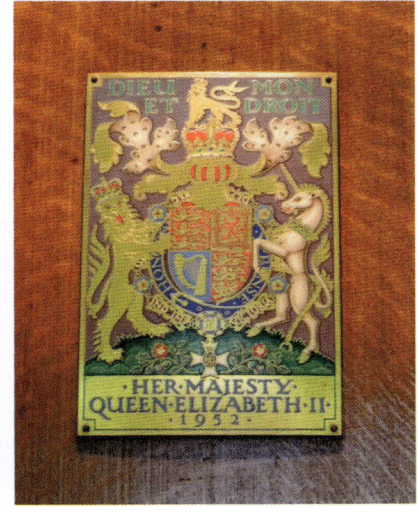

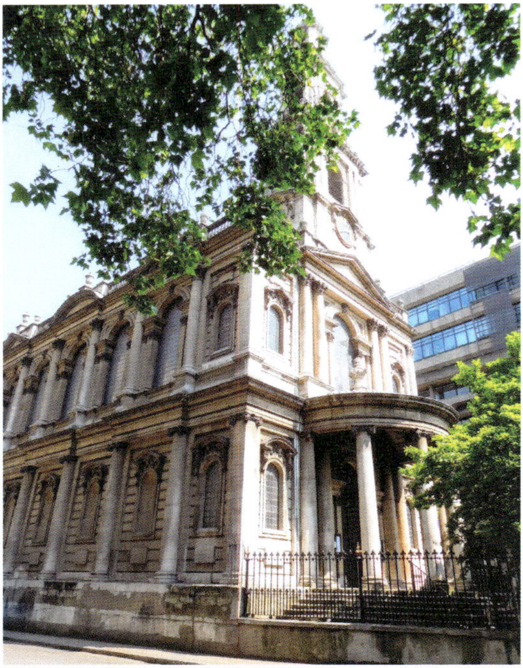

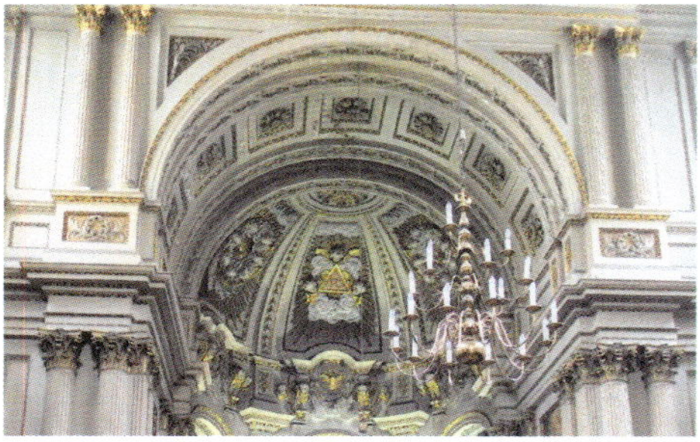

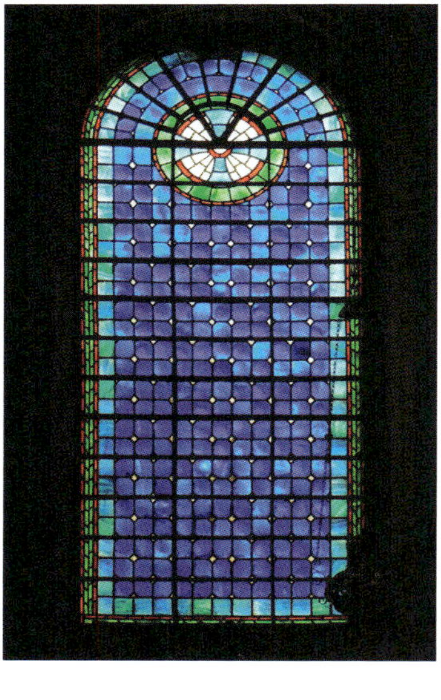

St. Mary-le-Strand

Location: Strand
Closest Underground Stations: Temple, Covent Garden
Nearby Attractions: The Strand, Somerset House, London Transport Museum
Hours: 11am-4pm Tues.-Thurs., closed Mon., Fri., Sat.

THIS IS OFTEN SAID TO BE THE FINEST BAROQUE CHURCH IN ALL OF LONDON and one of the city's most distinctive landmarks. The charming church is small and sits on a tiny island in the middle of the Strand, one of the busiest streets in the city. But yet they somehow managed to find a little plot to plant shade trees in front of the church. Traffic whizzes by on both sides and it can be challenging to cross the street to get there. But even so it's remarkably quiet inside because it was designed without windows in the back half where the entrance is located.

The church has stood here for almost three hundred years and is the official church of the Women's Royal Naval Service. You can peruse their book of remembrances for members who died in service. The building was designed by James Gibbs (1682-1754) and completed in 1723. Gibbs, who also designed St. Martin-in-the-Fields, was trained as an architect in Rome and many of the church's architectural elements are based on the churches in Rome that he studied. There are beautiful carvings of fruit, garlands and cherubs, and its tower looks like a three-tiered wedding cake. The interior is brilliantly white and has a magnificent white and gold barrel-vaulted ceiling.

St. Mary's also operates a church school, St. Clement Danes, not far away on Drury Lane. Like the church, the school has been in existence for 300 years. It teaches children from diverse backgrounds who typically speak at least 20 different languages.

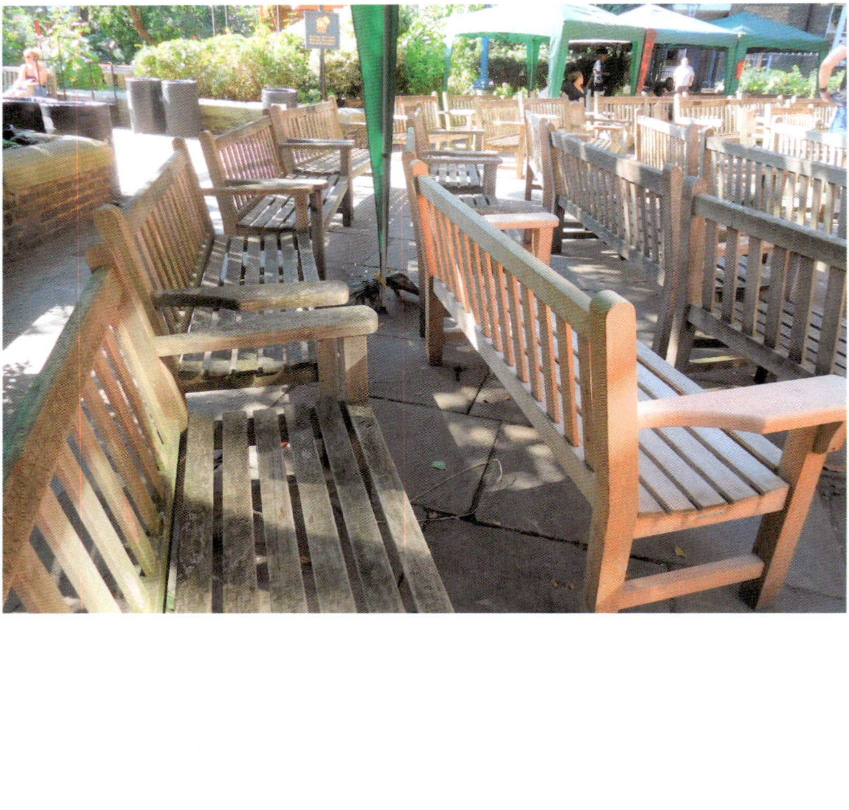

St. Paul's Church

Location: Bedford Street
Closest Underground Station: Covent Garden
Nearby Attractions: National Gallery, the Strand, Royal Opera House, Chinatown

Not to be confused with St. Paul's Cathedral, St. Paul's Church, located on Bedford Street just off Covent Garden, is also called "The Actors' Church". It has a long association with the theater, dating back to the 17th century when Covent Garden became the center of London's theater district. The tradition continues today.

A wide variety of plays, operas and concert events are held inside the church building throughout the year, and it is home to the Iris Theater Company. It also hosts memorial services for members of the theater community and their plaques line the walls—Vivien Leigh, Charlie Chaplin, Boris Karloff, Noel Coward and many more. In 2002, St. Paul's hosted the wedding of Gwen Stefani and Gavin Rossdale.

The church was designed and built by Inigo Jones in 1633. The side of the building facing the Covent Garden piazza looks like a Roman temple with four majestic stone columns under a massive portico. It's easy to mistake this side for the front of the church, but the "door" is false and is occupied by the altar on the interior side. Street acts take place in the piazza, cheered on by crowds of onlookers. And the first recorded performance of Punch and Judy took place under the church's portico in 1662.

Go around to the "back" of the church and you will find not only the entrance to the building itself but an award-winning garden and courtyard filled with people enjoying the solitude. Wooden benches commemorate famous people of the area and this is a favorite lunch time getaway from the crowds swarming Covent Garden. It's lovely, but it closes early, at 4:00 pm.

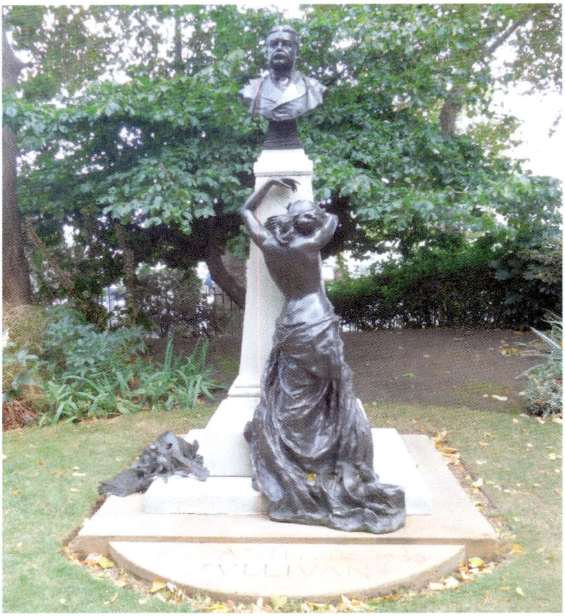

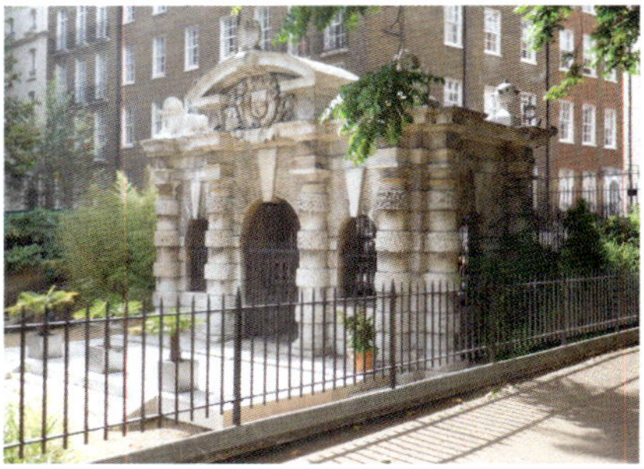

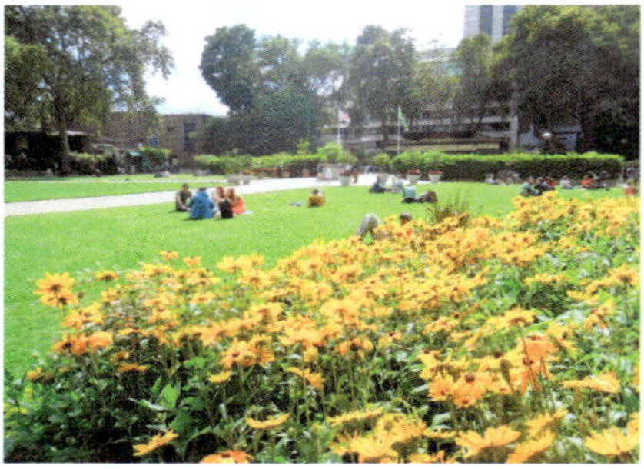

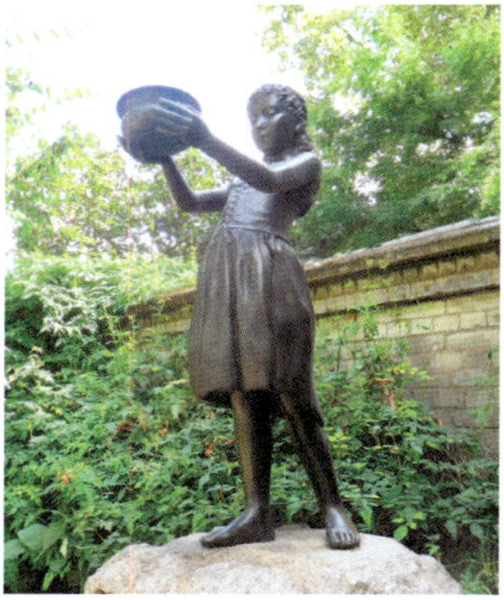

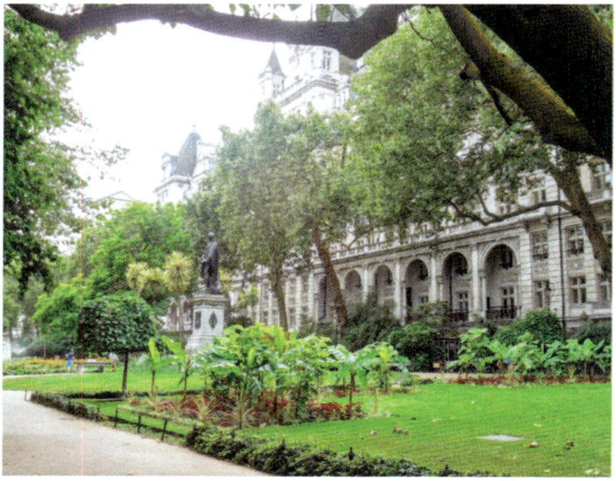

Victoria Embankment Gardens

Location: Victoria Embankment between Waterloo Bridge and Hungerford Bridge
Closest Underground Station: Embankment
Nearby Attractions: National Gallery, Trafalgar Square, Somerset House, Savoy Chapel

THESE GARDENS ARE ACTUALLY A CHAIN OF THREE GARDENS along the Thames' embankment, the Temple Gardens, Victoria Embankment Gardens, and Whitehall Gardens. The gardens total 37 acres and the main section runs parallel to the river between Waterloo Bridge and Hungerford Bridge.

Special features include stone fountains and water gardens, a bandstand and open-air theater which offers free concerts during the summertime, and a restaurant with outside seating. Ping pong tables have been set up for patrons of the park, and there's a 1.4 km fitness route from the Middle Temple Gardens to Victoria Embankment Gardens. Throughout are elegant pathways abundant with mature plane trees, shrubs that flower in the springtime and meticulous cut beds of seasonal flowers.

Sir Christopher Wren was the first to suggest a river embankment after the great fire of 1666, not only to beautify the riverfront but also to ease traffic congestion and house the main sewer. There was considerable opposition to the idea from business interests and this held up progress, but finally in 1864 work began.

Among the numerous statues and monuments is an especially dramatic memorial dedicated to Sir Arthur Sullivan who produced many operettas with his frequent collaborator, W. S. Gilbert. Under the bust of Sullivan is the crying Muse of Music who is so distraught that her clothes are falling off as she dramatically leans in mourning against the pedestal. At the bottom of the pedestal is a mask of Pan, companion to the nymphs, sheet music and a mandolin inscribed with the name of the sculptor, William Goscombe. It is fitting that the memorial faces the Savoy Hotel which was built using profits from Gilbert and Sullivan's shows. There are also many other impressive statues and memorials, including Lady Isabella Henry Somerset, President of the Woman's Temperance Association from 1890-1903; William Tyndale (c1484-1536), the first person to produce an English translation of the Bible; and Robert Burns, the national poet of Scotland.

Photo by Richard Smith, Bowen Island, Canada

Bloomsbury Square

Location: Bloomsbury Place, Bloomsbury
Closest Underground Station: Holborn
Nearby Attractions: British Museum, Sir John Soane's Museum
Hours: 7:30 am to dusk

This square was developed in the late 17th century and is one of the earliest London squares. It is not far from the British Museum. Today most of the buildings surrounding the square are used as offices, but at one time it was lined with terraced houses occupied by members of the gentry.

None of the original 17th century houses survive, but there are many from the 18th and 19th centuries. Le Cordon Bleu currently occupies number 15, and in 1902 Gertrude Stein lived at number 40. In the musical rendition of *Oliver!*, Mr. Brownlow, Oliver's benefactor, lives in Bloomsbury Square.

Within the square itself are winding walkways lined with benches and a small playground for the children. There also is an impressive statue of Charles James Fox, a colleague of the Dukes of Bedford who at the time owned Bedford House and most of the north side of the square. Today, Bedford House is home to the Bedford Place Apartments which offers tourists self-catering rentals as a hotel alternative.

Photo by Schaier

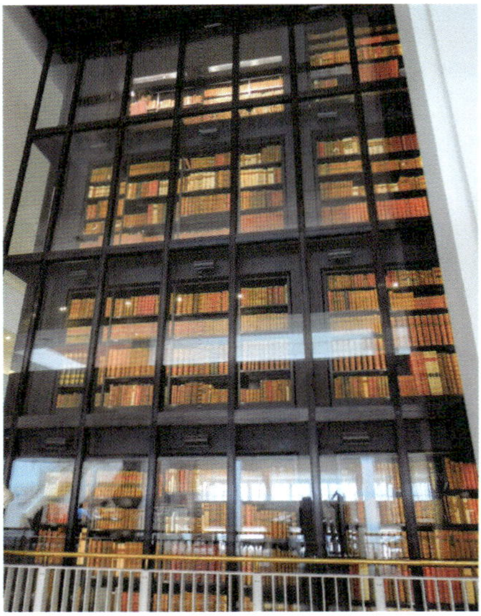

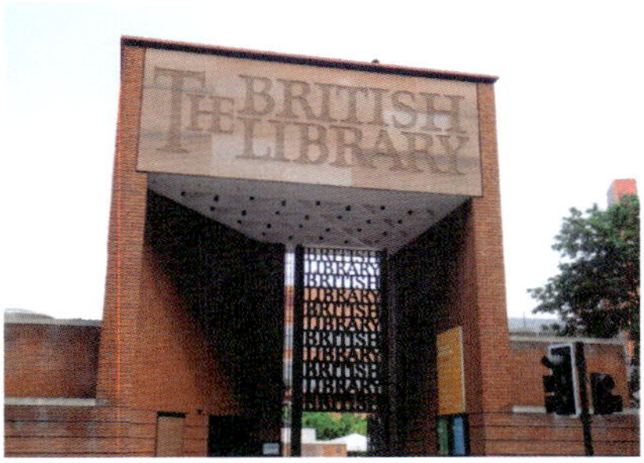
THE BRITISH LIBRARY

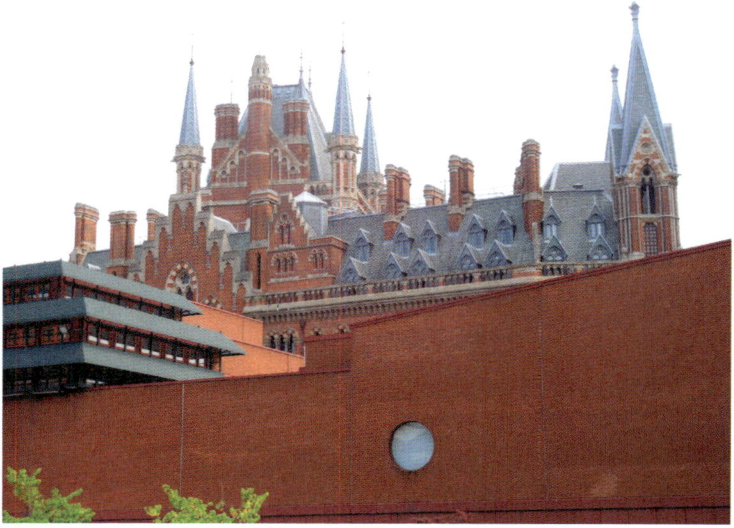

British Library

Location: 96 Euston Road
Closest Underground Station: King's Cross St. Pancras
Hours: 9:30am-6pm Mon.-Fri., 9:30am-5pm Sat., 11am-5pm Sun.

BRITAIN'S MAJOR CONTRIBUTION TO WESTERN CIVILIZATION IS THE WRITTEN WORD. The new state-of-the-art library building built in 1997 is a fitting tribute to that remarkable distinction.

There are 150 million items in the library—every published book, manuscript and map in Britain and Ireland is housed here. In 1823, King George III gifted 65,000 books to the library with the stipulation that they remain on display for all to see. A high-tech six-story glass tower has been designed to hold them. They are inaccessible to the public but you can get a good view on the second level behind the information desk.

Two spectacular rooms in the Sir John Ritblat Gallery contain treasures of Western civilization. These include Bibles (both the *Gutenberg Bible* and the *Lindisfarne Gospels* from AD 698 with their illustrations by monks), Shakespeare's *Hamlet*, Lewis Carroll's *Alice's Adventures in Wonderland*, the *Magna Carta* (the 1215 basis for England's constitutional system of government), Chaucer's *Canterbury Tales*, Beatles' lyrics scribbled on a greeting card, and some of da Vinci's sketches. You can examine every page of these rare historic works and read supporting material by the curators on screens located near the displays. The rooms in which these treasures are housed are dimly lit because of their extreme sensitivity to light, and photos are not allowed.

The entry courtyard is an appealing place. There is a large statue of Isaac Newton here who is holding a compass to measure the universe. Here also you will find an outdoor cafe with beautiful views of the Victorian building housing the St. Pancras railway station next door.

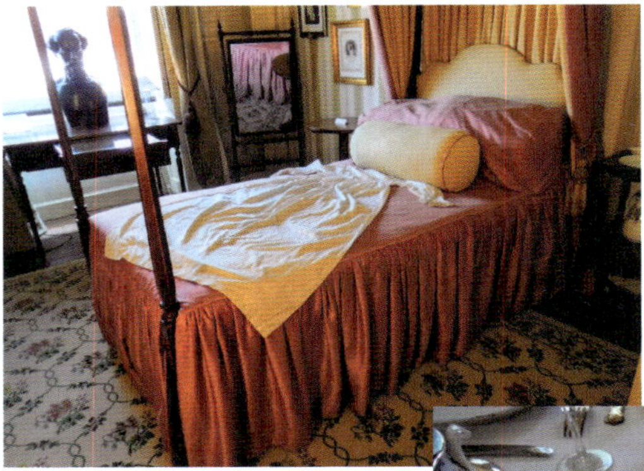

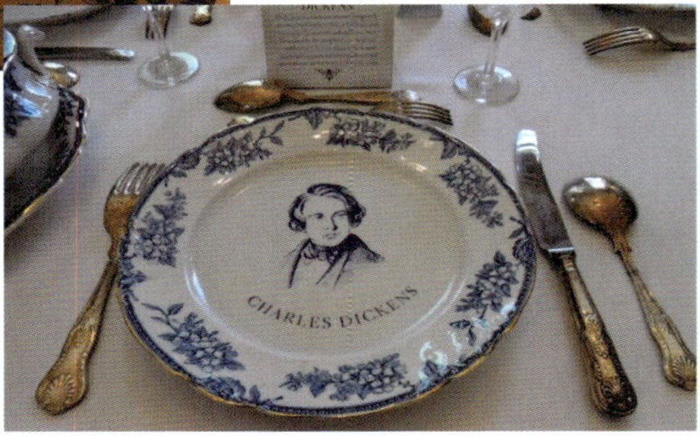
CHARLES DICKENS

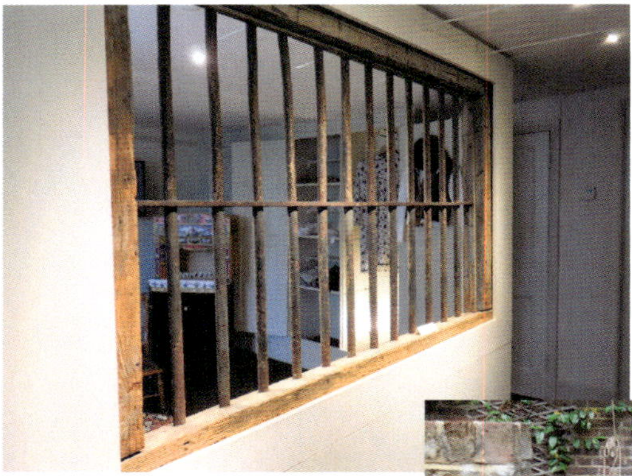

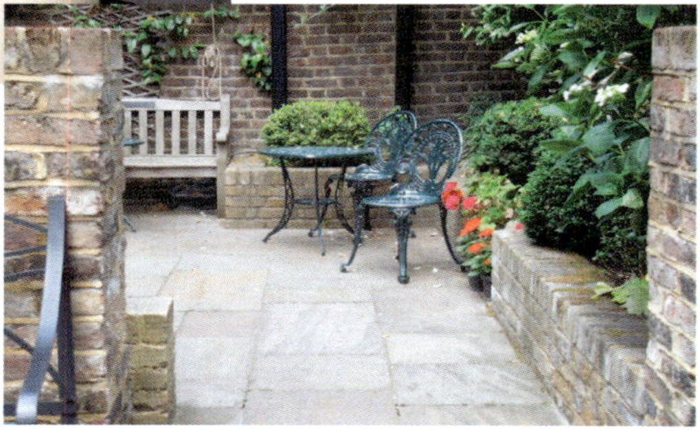

CHARLES DICKENS MUSEUM

Location: 48 Doughty Street
Closest Underground Stations: Russell Square, Chancery Lane
Nearby Attractions: British Museum, Russell Square, Foundling Museum
Hours: 10am-5pm Tues.-Sun., closed Mon.

THIS IS A CHARMING LITTLE MUSEUM that explores Dickens' work and family life, and captures the essence of the author who addressed the social ills of Victorian society in his fiction. The writer lived here when he wrote *Oliver Twist* and *Nicholas Nickleby* and finished the *Pickwick Papers* standing up at a tall clerk's desk. The desk that you see in this house is where he wrote many of his later works including *A Tale of Two Cities* and *Great Expectations*. It stood in the bay window of his home at Gad's Hill Place overlooking the front lawn.

The house contains handwritten drafts, first editions, letters and rooms that look exactly as they would have when he lived here. An especially touching item is his young wife's engagement ring. And in the room where his children slept and played is a wall with a section of prison bars from the debtors' prison where a young Dickens and his family were forced to live due to his father's dire finances.

You are also able to tour the laundry scrub room downstairs in the servants' quarters, the couple's bedroom, and their dining room with the blue and white plate displaying Charles' name. In another room is a tiny bed set against a wall painted with quotes from several of his works including *The Pickwick Papers* and *David Copperfield*, and "Please sir, I want some more" from *Oliver Twist*.

The museum has an enchanting cafe and bar that serves light meals both in and out of doors. And not far away is a local pub that they recommend, The Lady Ottoline (at Northington Street, just a short walk south along Doughty Street). It has a strong Victorian feel and offers a discount on food to those with a Museum ticket or receipt.

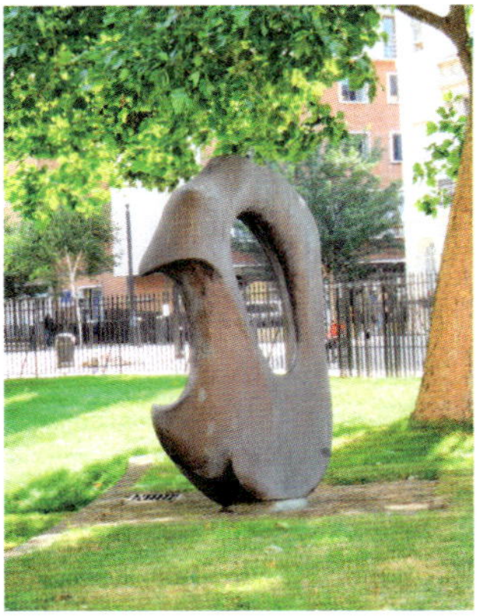

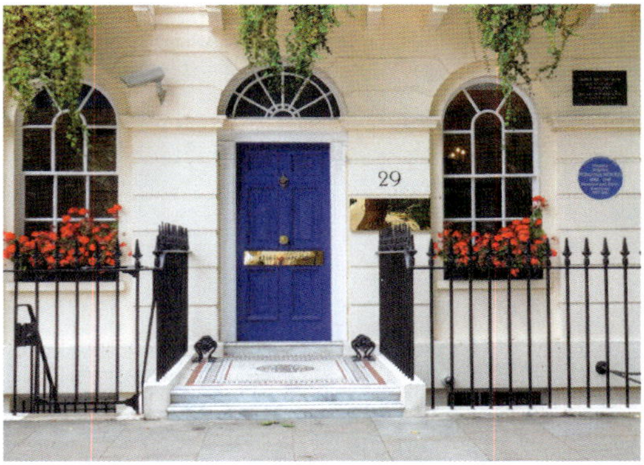
29

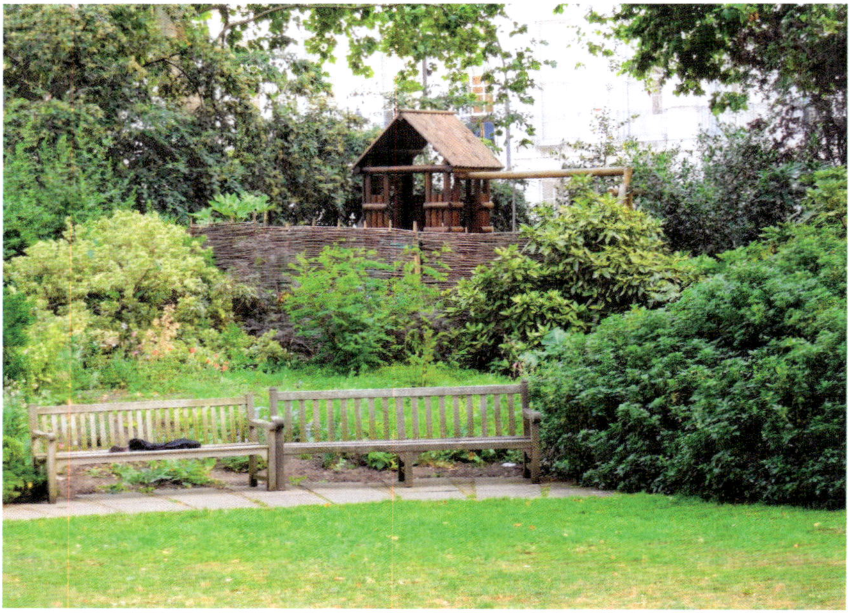

Fitzroy Square

Location: Fitzroy Street, south off Euston Road (Fitzrovia)
Closest Underground Stations: Warren Street, Great Portland Street
Nearby Attractions: Regent's Park, Pollock's Toy Museum

THIS IDYLLIC SQUARE IS A GRADE I LISTED MASTERPIECE that was designed in the late 18th century. It is a peaceful and quiet place in the northern part of London not far from Regent's Park.

Here you will find elegant Georgian homes where famous artists, writers and statesmen lived. Both Virginia Woolf and George Bernard Shaw lived at number 29—not at the same time; it has a beautiful blue door, tile stoop, and frontage overlooking the park. Stroll around the square and notice the buildings and plaques, then take a seat on a quiet bench and enjoy the lush greenery and birds.

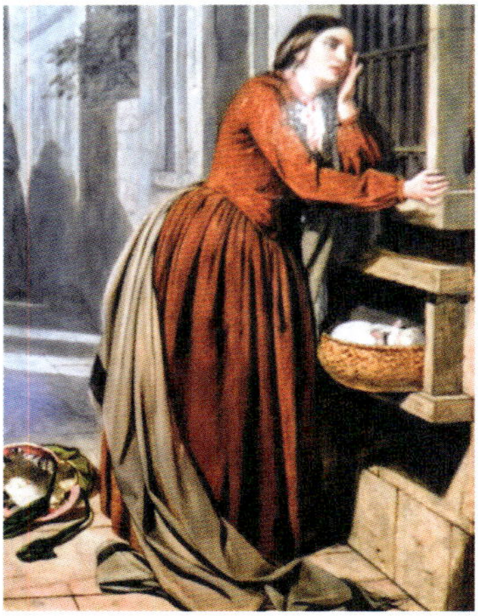

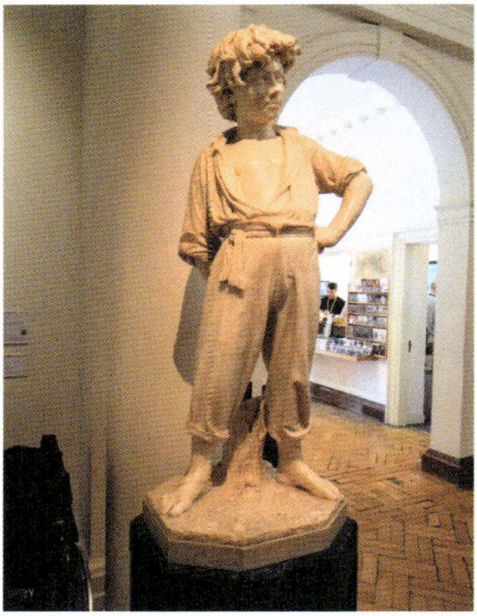

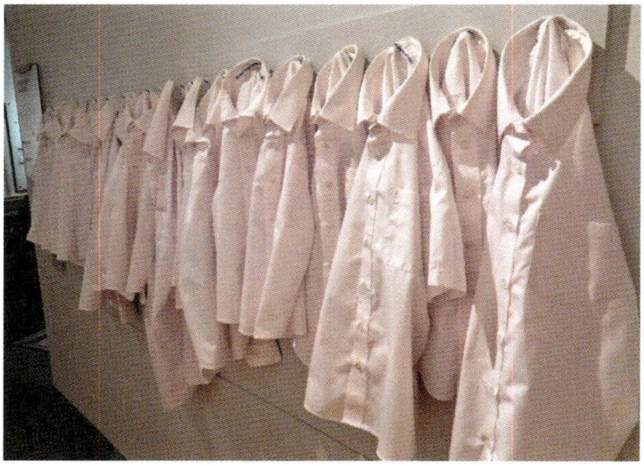

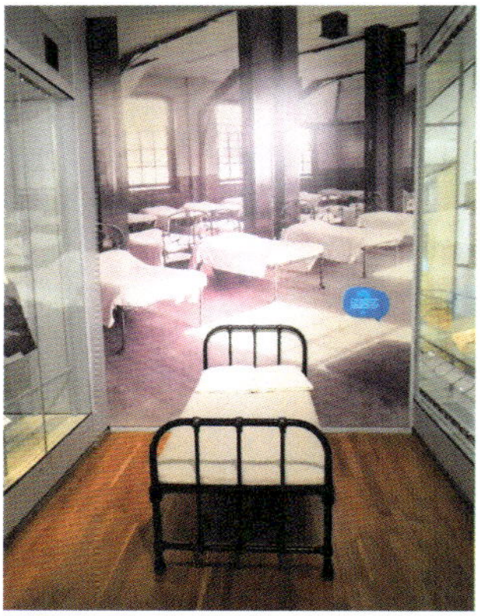

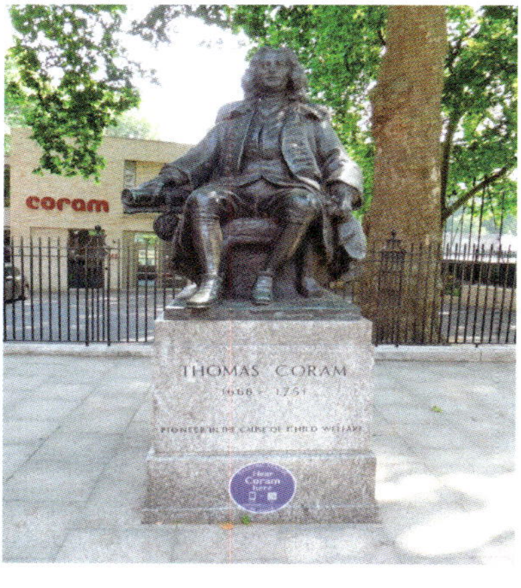
coram
THOMAS CORAM

Foundling Museum

Location: 40 Brunswick Square
Closest Underground Stations: Russell Square, King's Cross St Pancras, Euston
Nearby Attractions: British Museum, Russell Square, Charles Dickens Museum
Open: 10am-5pm Tues.-Sat., 11am-5pm Sun., closed Mon.

THIS USED TO BE A HOME FOR ABANDONED CHILDREN where poor little ones were cared for and nurtured. See the grief on the faces of widows, women who had been deserted by the child's father, or those with an illegitimate child as they made the agonizing decision to drop off their child for the prospect of a better life. But then rejoice in the smiles on the faces of the foundlings as they mix up a batch of bread dough with their new friends.

The building housing the museum was at one time a hospital, home for foundlings and gallery for fine art due to the generosity of Captain Thomas Coram and his colleagues, the artist William Hogarth and the composer George Frederick Handel. Together in 1739 these three men founded the hospital with the purpose of housing, educating and placing the foundlings in private homes. The art museum was started with paintings donated by Hogarth and other artists followed suit, creating Britain's first art museum and a nationally important collection of 18th century paintings, sculpture and furniture. The idea was that couples would come to see the art work and take home a child. The hospital operated on this site from 1745 to 1926. Today it continues as the children's charity Coram.

The museum is very active, hosting concerts, special exhibitions, artists' projects and talks. A recent artists' project called *Labelled* explores young peoples' experiences of being labeled as a "child in care". This exhibit consists of a line-up of twenty or so identical white shirts in varying sizes, tightly hung together on nails and beautiful in its poignant simplicity.

Adjacent to the museum are Coram Fields, with several children's' playgrounds for different age groups, a sandpit and a small petting zoo. Adults must be accompanied by a child in order to gain admittance.

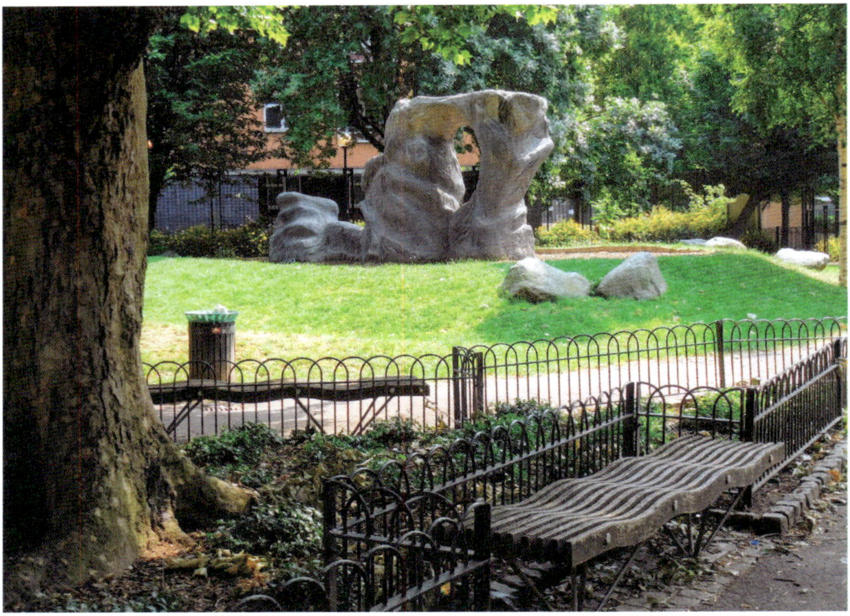

JUDD STREET OPEN SPACE

Location: Judd Street/Cromer Street
Closest Underground Stations: St. Pancras Station, King's Cross Station
Nearby Attractions: British Library, Regent's Park, Madame Tussaud's

THE NAME COULDN'T MAKE IT ANY CLEARER: this is an "open space" and it's on Judd Street. Located in the Camden area of London, it was re-landscaped recently and now includes new gates with a leaf motif and an exercise area for dogs. Adjacent to the small park is the Church of the Holy Cross whose mission is to care for "those who experience the ravages of life".

You won't find other tourists here, but you will find benches, lawns, an old plane tree, winding paths and a wooden "zoo" for toddlers.

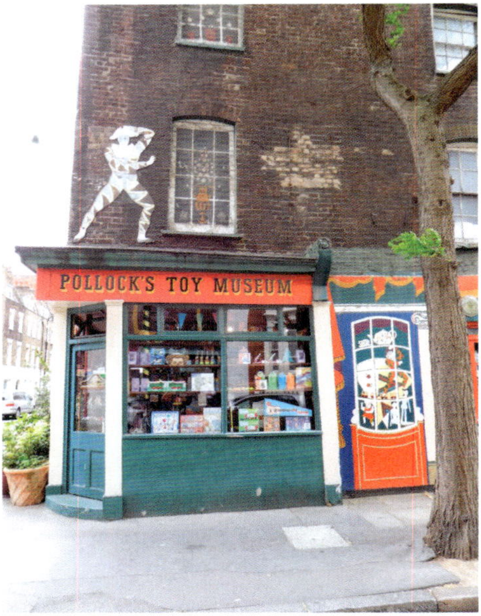
POLLOCK'S TOY MUSEUM

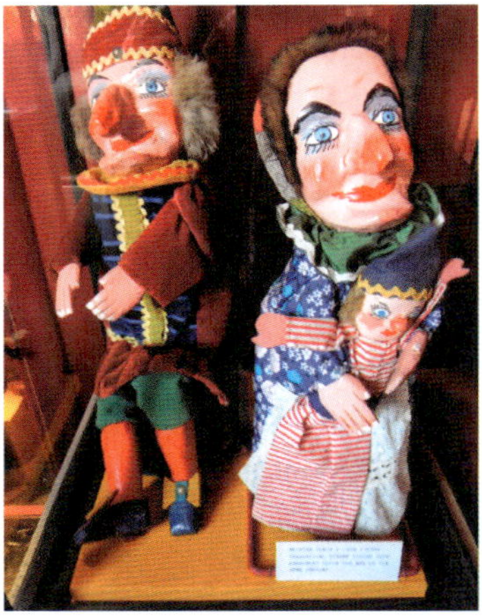

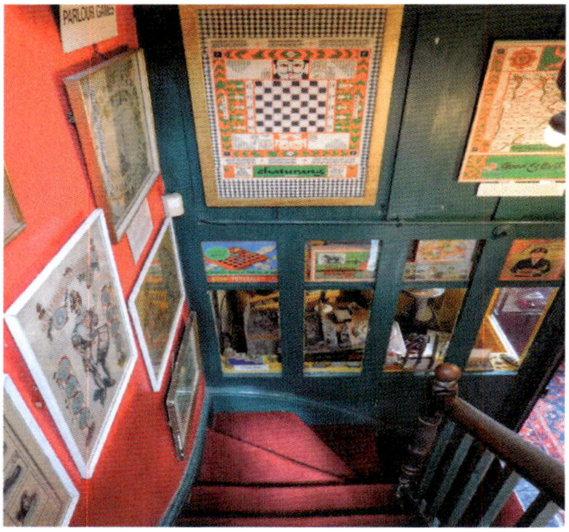
PARLOUS GAMES

Pollock's Toy Museum

Location: 1 Scala Street
Closest Underground Stations: Goodge Street, Warren Street
Nearby Attractions: British Museum, Russell Square, Fitzroy Square
Hours: 10am-5pm Mon.-Sat., closed Sun.

THIS DELIGHTFUL FIND CAN'T HELP BUT MAKE YOU SMILE. It has a fanciful painted facade and is inside a small old house, spread out over several floors and connected by tiny winding staircases. Toys, dolls, matchbox cars, puppets and games from the 19th and early 20th centuries are artfully displayed in glass cases, and it is sure to bring back memories for 50-somethings and older. There also is a toy store at the end of the self-guided tour which will please the young ones.

Stories are included on wooden paddles next to the displays. The story of the teddy bear is particularly enchanting. This toy was developed in 1902 and named after Theodore Roosevelt who refused to kill a bear cub while on a hunting trip with some colleagues. Word spread, a political cartoon appeared in the Washington Post, the future founder of Ideal Toys started manufacturing it, and it became very popular. This was a toy well suited to the times, for it could be manufactured during WWI without using materials needed for the war effort, boys were not embarassed to play with this "doll", and it was approved by child development experts because it was soft and huggable.

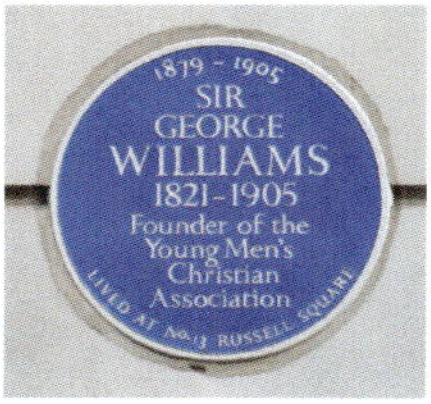
1879 - 1905
SIR
GEORGE
WILLIAMS
1821-1905
Founder of the
Young Men's
Christian
Association
LIVED AT No.13 RUSSELL SQUARE

Russell Square

Location: Guilford Street, Bloomsbury
Closest Underground Station: Russell Square
Nearby Attractions: British Museum, University of London, Foundling Museum

RUSSELL SQUARE IS A LARGE GARDEN SQUARE IN BLOOMSBURY and a stone's throw from the British Museum. It's lined with handsome houses owned by the upper middle classes and buildings belonging to the University of London. Also, at 1-8 Russell Square is the grande dame Hotel Russell, a listed historic landmark that originally opened in 1898.

There is another listed building on the square that is interesting and unique. It's small—not much bigger than a garden shed—and painted dark green. This is a Victorian cabman's shelter and one of only thirteen that still exist throughout the city.

Today the cabman's shelter is used as a snack bar, but when they were built in the late 19th century, they were meant to provide "wholesome refreshments at moderate prices" for drivers of hansom cabs and hackney carriages who were not allowed to leave their cabs when parked at a cab stand. In 1874, a fund was established, shelters were built on the roadsides, and cab drivers could stop by for a nourishing meal. Although the shelters were restricted by police regulations to the size of a horse and cart, they managed to squeeze in a tiny kitchen and seating for ten to thirteen cab drivers. Books and newspapers were provided by local benefactors, and gambling, drinking and swearing were prohibited.

In the square, you will find benches, peaceful walkways, statues and an ornamental fountain. Near one of the entrances is a reasonably priced year-round café/restaurant that serves people on their way to work and tourists going to or returning from the British Museum. This is a good spot to wind down after a day at the museum.

[64]

St. Pancras Parish Church

Location: Euston Road (Bloomsbury, Camden)
Closest Underground Station: Euston
Nearby attractions: British Library, Regent's Park, University College
Open: 8am-6pm Mon.-Thurs.

𝕴 THOUGHT FOR A MOMENT I WAS IN GREECE. I was walking down Euston Road in Bloomsbury heading for St. Pancras and four large draped female figures supporting an entablature similar to what you would see at the Acropolis in Athens caught my eye. The designers of St. Pancras admired Athenian architecture and designed this interesting church in the Greek revival style, abundant with columns, cornices, gables and pediments. The draped women are a prominent feature of the exterior. They are located above the crypt on both sides of the entrance and are holding extinguished torches and empty jugs, appropriate to their positions as guardians of the dead.

St. Pancras also has interesting sculptures in the gardens on the sides of the church. A recent exhibit entitled *Alien* consisted of bronze casts of giant aliens in human form.

The parish of this church is one of the oldest in England, possibly dating from Roman times. The present building was inaugurated in 1822 and has a Grade I listing from English Heritage. It is dedicated to the boy soldier and Roman martyr, St. Pancras.

With seating for 600 people, the church is known for its outstanding music, art and sculpture, and has a full schedule of concerts, recitals and lectures. The Crypt over which the four women outside stand guard is atmospheric and used for art exhibitions, performances, filming and book launches. There are free lunchtime recitals in the sanctuary on Thursdays at 1:15 and choral evensong on Sundays at 6:00 pm.

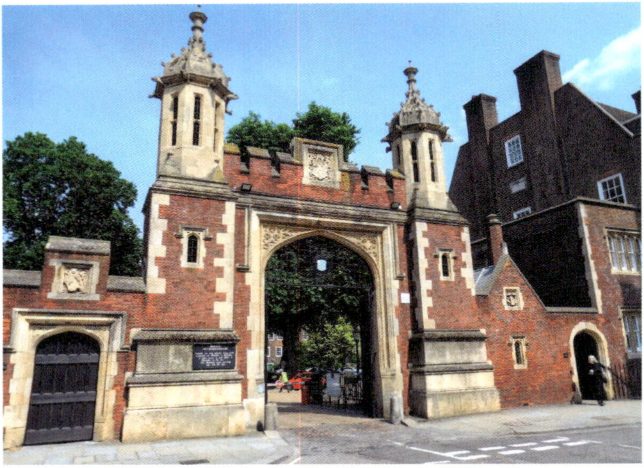

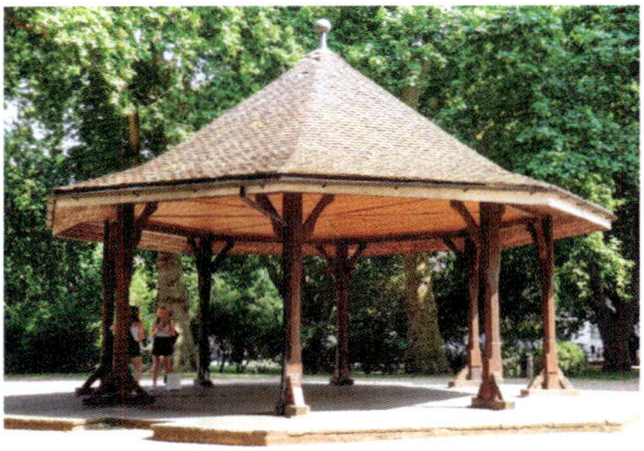

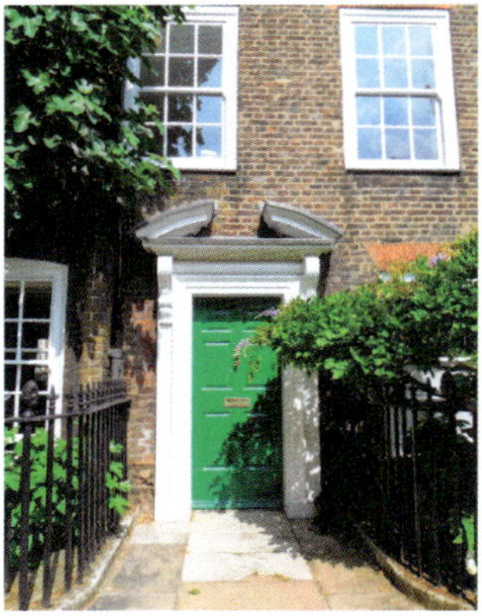

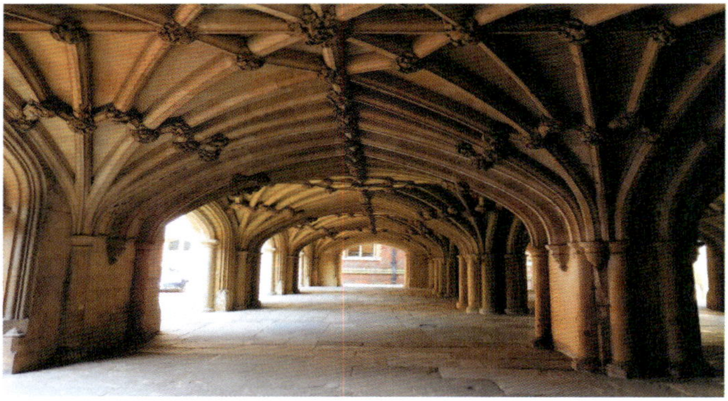

Lincoln's Inn and Lincoln's Inn Fields

Location: Between Chancery Lane and Lincoln's Inn Fields, Camden
Closest Underground Stations: Holborn, Chancery Lane
Nearby attractions: British Museum

𝔄T FIRST, THIS PLACE CONFUSED ME BECAUSE IT REFERS TO MEDIEVAL DEFINITIONS. An "inn" is a residence for students (law students if it is an Inn of Court as in this case). Today, it also includes lawyers and judges. The term "fields" is meant to indicate a public square.

Lincoln's Inn sits on 11 acres and houses the Honourable Society of Lincoln's Inn, an amalgam of judges, barristers and law students whose goal is to improve their skills, professionalism and ethics. The society has been in existence since the 14th century and is one of the most prestigious in the world.

Lincoln's Inn resembles the campuses of Oxford and Cambridge but it is smaller. You enter the walled square on Chancery Lane through a Tudor brick gatehouse dating from 1517. Around the square you will find 19th century buildings that mainly are used to house small law firms, a convenient location since it is close to the Royal Courts of Justice. There also is a 15th century chapel remodeled in 1620 by Inigo Jones, and a Great Hall and Library, both dating from 1843. The Old Hall is the finest building in the Inn and, indeed, in all of London. It is small but beautifully proportioned and executed, and dates from 1490.

The "fields" are the public square adjacent to the Inn and designed in the 1630's by Inigo Jones. This is the largest public square in London and is where at one time public executions were held. It is wide open, tree lined and atmospheric and has an old pavilion not far from the gatehouse. There are also some lovely old buildings surrounding the square. The oldest is Lindsey House at 59–60 Lincoln's Inn Fields, which was built in 1640 and has been attributed to Inigo Jones. And Sir John Soane's Museum dates from 1812 and is at 13 Lincoln's Inn Fields.

[68]

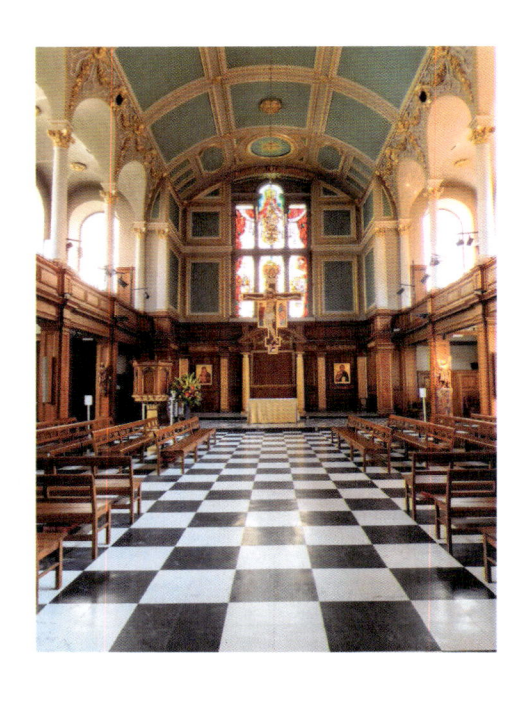

St. Andrew Holborn Church

Location: 5 St. Andrew Street, Holborn
Closest Underground Station: Chancery Lane
Nearby attractions: British Museum, St. Paul's Cathedral, Embankment gardens
Open: 9am-5pm Mon.-Fri.

It's on a busy street but I was attracted to the small colorful gardens which in 2015 won *Best New Public Space* at the London Planning Awards. That was the year they officially opened to allow easier access to the west end of the church. I also was drawn in by the charming blewcoat statues mounted above the door, indicative of the charity school that operated here in the 19th century.

This has been a site of worship for at least 1000 years. The present structure dates from 1687 when Christopher Wren, a leading architect of the time, rebuilt the church on roughly the same ground as its medieval predecessor. It is the largest of the 52 parish churches that Wren designed.

The interior of the church was rebuilt in 1961 as a Guild Church. A guild church is designed to serve the local working community, has no congregation per se and holds no Sunday services. Instead, it offers Holy Communion on weekdays at lunchtime for local office workers, and morning and evening prayers on Tuesdays through Thursdays. To raise money, it hires out its space for events and offers services such as charity administration, financial management, events management, and grants distribution.

Several notables have been affiliated with the church including 18th century philanthropist Thomas Coram who created the London Foundling Hospital and whose tomb has been situated at St Andrew's since the 1920s.

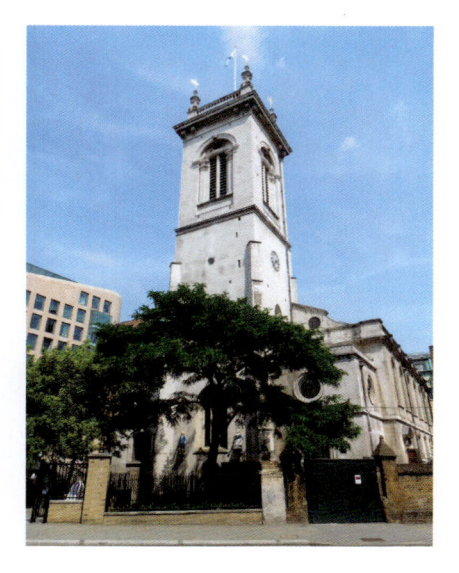

MUSEUM
Art Fund_
Museum of
the Year 2017
Finalist
WE ARE
A FINALIST

Sir John Soane's Museum

Location: 12-14 Lincoln's Inn Fields
Closest Underground Stations: Holborn, Chancery Lane
Nearby attractions: British Museum, Lincoln's Inn
Hours: 10am-5pm Tues.-Sat., closed Sun.-Mon.
Admission: Free

THIS HOUSE-MUSEUM IS AN ARCHITECT'S NIRVANA. It's on a square, Lincoln's Inn Fields, and was built in 1808-1812. Sir John Soane (1753-1837) lived here and established it as a museum in 1833.

Soane was a professor of architecture at the Royal Academy who specialized in the Neo-Classical style and is mainly known for his design of the Bank of England. He intended his collection to be used for research and teaching and thereby inspire architectural students, and the *Oxford Dictionary of Architecture* describes it as "one of the most complex, intricate, and ingenious series of interiors ever conceived".

Most of the museum has been kept as it was at the time of Sir John's death 180 years ago. In the basement rooms, hundreds of busts, masks and broken statues stare out at you, and urns, friezes, arches, columns, and broken architectural fragments cover every surface. It is crowded and claustrophobic even though there are plenty of skylights and artificial lighting, and you have to be careful not to disturb anything.

Upstairs, the Model Room contains very fine architectural models of ancient Greek monuments and some of Soane's own buildings. In the main red and green room on the ground floor are many mirrors that fool the eyes, and the split level floor is disorienting. Throughout you will find knickknacks, chairs, lamps, tables, sculptures, and paintings.

After touring the house, you may enjoy the tranquil gardens in the courtyard that are connected to the museum with a below-streetlevel passageway.

[72]

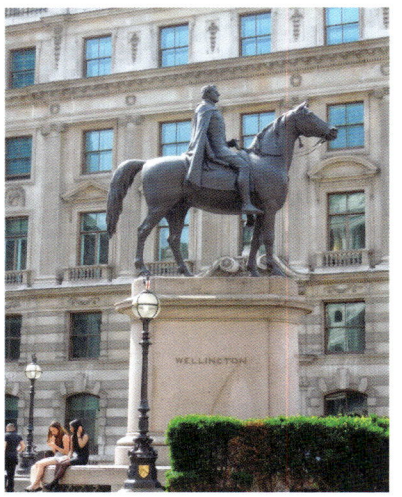

Bank of England Museum

Location: Enter from Bartholomew Lane
Closest Underground Station: Bank
Nearby attractions: St. Paul's, the Guildhall, Leadenhall Market
Hours: 10am-5pm Mon.-Fri., closed Sat.-Sun.
Admission: Free

THIS IS WHERE YOU CAN TEST YOUR BRAWN AND YOUR BRAIN. Try to pick up with one hand a 28-pound gold ingot worth $500,000, or take a turn at running the economy and setting interest rates to a level at which the "ideal" 2% inflation rate is met. See how hard it is.

The Bank of England has been England's central bank since 1694. It manages the national debt, lends to other banks, and regulates the country's banking system, similar to what the Federal Reserve does in the U.S.. To do its job, it works with the government to set interest rates, print money, and house stacks of gold bars.

The museum traces the Bank's history. You will find banknotes from 1699 to the present, an old safe, account books, silver artifacts, and a Roman mosaic floor. You can also admire the security features that are used to protect against the counterfeiting of bank notes. But the highlight is under the rotunda in the central trading hall—the real gold bar mentioned above that is worth about $500,000. You can hold it under the watchful eyes of security guards.

The building was designed by Sir John Soane in 1788, but most of it was rebuilt in the years between 1925 and 1939. The windowless walls are all that remain of the original building. On the square opposite the Bank is a magnificent equestrian statue of British soldier and statesman, the Duke of Wellington (1769-1852).

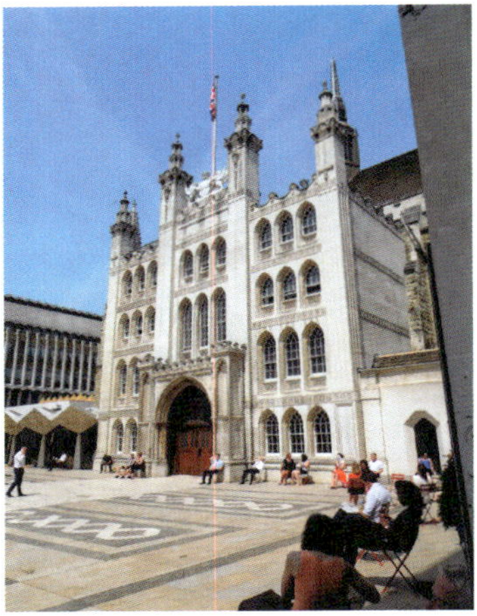

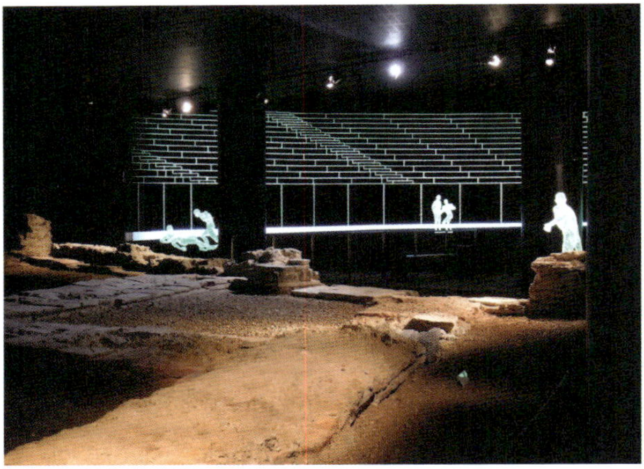

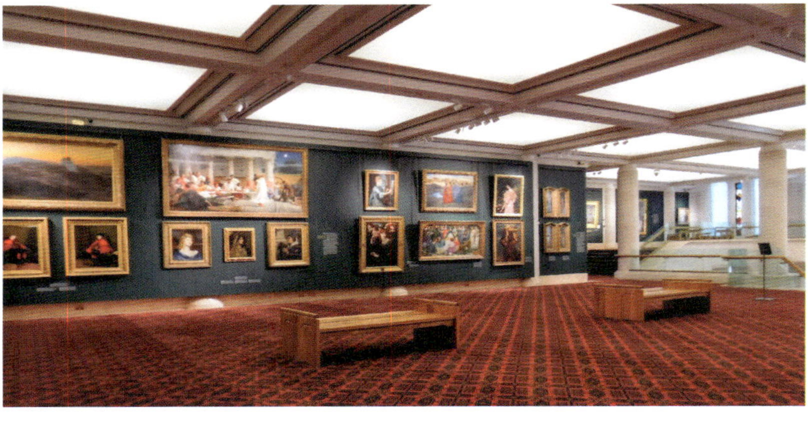

GUILDHALL ART GALLERY

Location: Guildhall Yard (off Gresham Street), The City
Closest Underground Stations: Bank, St. Paul's
Nearby attractions: St. Paul's Cathedral, Bank of England, St. Stephen Walbrook
Hours: 10am-5pm Mon.-Sat., noon-4pm Sun.
Admission: free

IT WAS A WARM SUMMER DAY AND THE BEAUTIFUL COURTYARD IN FRONT of the 15th century guildhall was filled with office workers having their lunches. I walked into the adjacent art gallery and was mesmerized. The temperature was cool and felt great after the heat outdoors, soft music was playing in the background, beautiful art surrounded me and I had the place to myself.

The Guildhall Art Gallery is home to Britain's biggest painting, John Singleton Copley's *Defeat of Floating Batteries at Gibraltar* covering the two-story wall at the farthest end of the main room. Downstairs at the base of Copley's work is a poignant temporary exhibition created for the centenary of WWI.

The gallery's collection was established in 1886 and includes works dating from 1670 to the present. Portraits, pre-Raphaelite masterpieces, and a range of paintings documenting London's dramatic history are beautifully displayed in expansive, open and airy showrooms. The Victorian Galleries contain charming paintings of London scenes.

In the basement are ruins of an 1,800 year-old Roman amphitheater which was discovered when the gallery was being built. It is said to have held 6,000 spectators who watched executions, animal fights, and gladiatorial combat. On the square above, laid out in Guildhall Yard, is a circular outline of what once was the perimeter of the amphitheater.

The Guildhall that sits on the courtyard has a fanciful facade, a grand medieval hall with coats of arms and banners, and plush banqueting halls. The building dates from 1411 and is where guilds met and amassed great wealth. Today it hosts about 100 professional associations and unions.

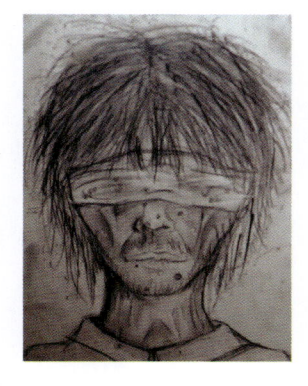

[76]

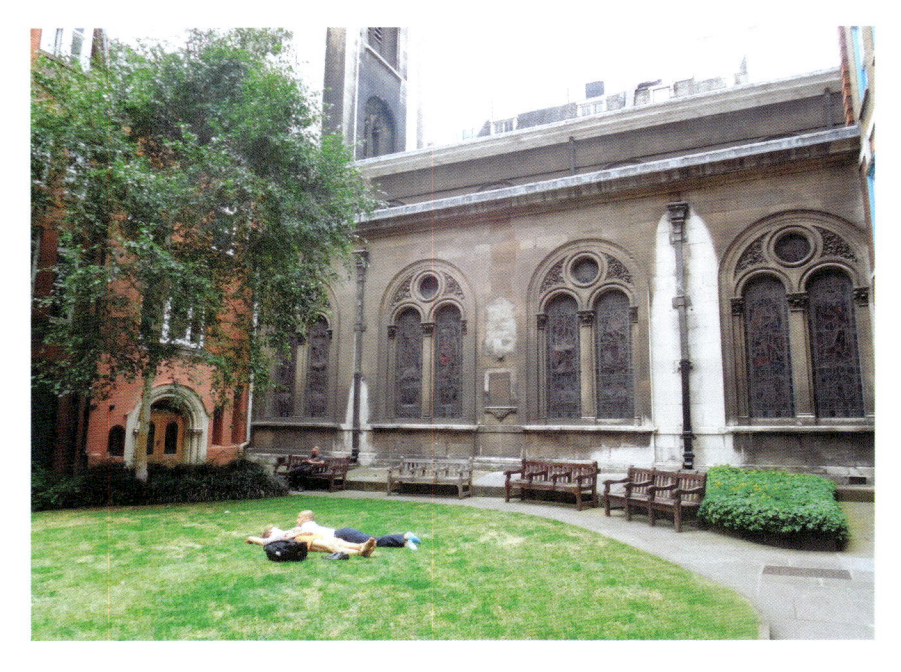

Garden of St. Michael's Cornhill

Location: Cornhill Street and St. Michael's Alley in the City borough
Closest Underground Stations: Bank, Monument
Nearby attractions: Leadenhall Market, Lloyd's of London building, Bank of England

As YOU WALK UP CORNHILL STREET HEADING TOWARD LEADENHALL MARKET and Lloyd's of London, a blue door on an extremely narrow church next to an even narrower alleyway will catch your eye on the right hand side of the street. This is the Parish Church of St. Michael Cornhill and it stands on one of the oldest Christian sites in Britain, dating back to the Roman occupation. The church was destroyed in the Great Fire of 1666 and was rebuilt by Sir Christopher Wren in 1672.

To get to the churchyard, walk down St. Michael's Alley to the corner, take a left at The Jamaica Wine House and go to the farthest gate. The churchyard is laid out as a garden with lawns, flower beds, shrubs and trees and is an enjoyable place to spend some time on one of the benches or stretched out on the lawn. It is very quiet here, except for the hum of low voices coming from the wine house.

A short distance up the street is the fabulous Lloyd's of London building. It is constructed of steel and built in the "inside-out" manner of Bowellism, a post-modern style made famous by the Pompidou Centre in Paris. Bowellist buildings are built so that the skeleton is exposed—all of the services and utilities that would typically be hidden in the core of the building are instead placed on the outside, displaying the innards in full splendor.

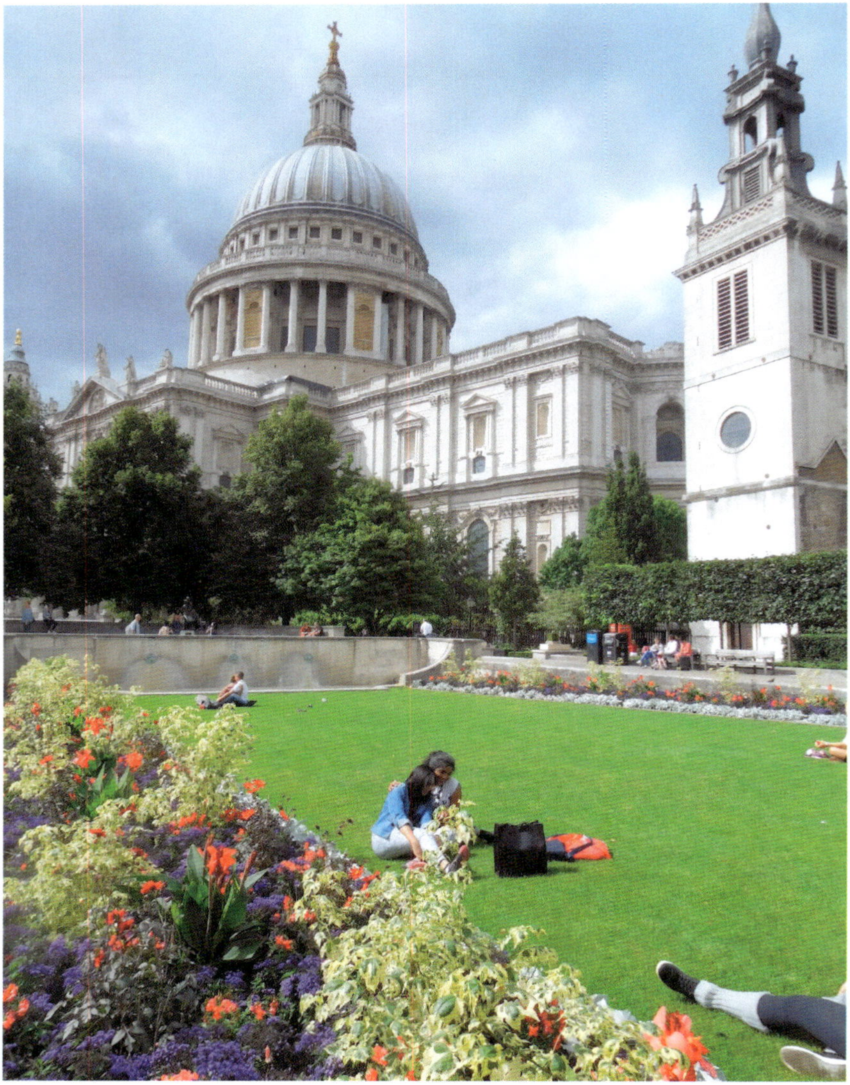

Courtyards of St. Paul's Cathedral

Location: Ludgate Hill
Closest Underground Station: St. Paul's
Nearby Attractions: Tate Modern, Shakespeare's Globe Theater, Guildhall Art Gallery
Hours: 8:30 am - 4:00 pm, evensong at 5:00 pm

FOR MORE THAN 1400 YEARS, a Cathedral dedicated to St. Paul has stood on this site. Over the centuries, it has been built and rebuilt five times. The existing building was completed in 1712 and is one of fifty-two churches built by Sir Christopher Wren following the Great Fire of London. It is an Anglican Church and the seat of the Bishop and Diocese of London.

An excellent audio tour is included with the pricey admission, and if you're lucky, you'll also catch a tour by one of the volunteers. To save the admission cost, go to evensong. Get in line about 4:30; you'll also have an opportunity to see the incredible interior, but you are not free to wander through the church before, during, or after evensong.

Inside the Cathedral building are astonishing mosaics, paintings, sculptures, carvings, Latin inscriptions, and tombs and memorials including one to Florence Nightingale and another to John Donne. There also is some outstanding modern art here. A pair of companion works that caught my eye consists of two stark white crosses on the right and left of the aisle leading into the nave. They were created in 2014 by Jewish artist and designer Gerry Judah and memorialize the dead of WWI. The crosses are mounted with the ruins of wrecked buildings, also in stark white so as to resemble the moments after bombing when everything is still covered in a white dust.

You can climb the 259 steps to the whispering gallery up above where the acoustics cause whispers to echo around the dome, and to the top of the dome itself, where you will be rewarded with amazing views of London. Some compare the view from here favorably to that from the London Eye.

After touring the Cathedral, you may want to sit down and relax in a peaceful place. Yet most visitors do not take the time to visit the side garden and the lovely churchyard of St. Paul's. One of these areas backs up to the side of the building and consists simply of grass and a few benches. The other is larger and more colorful—a pleasant space of lawns bordered with trees, benches and flower beds and it has a nice view of the cathedral and its dome in the background. People refresh themselves here after touring inside or climbing to the top of the Cathedral's dome.

[79]

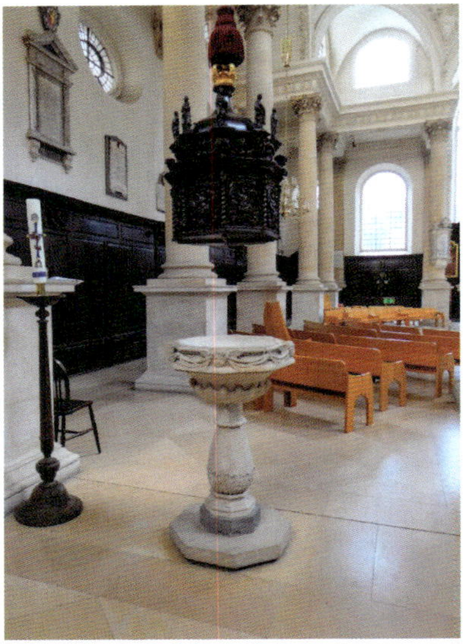

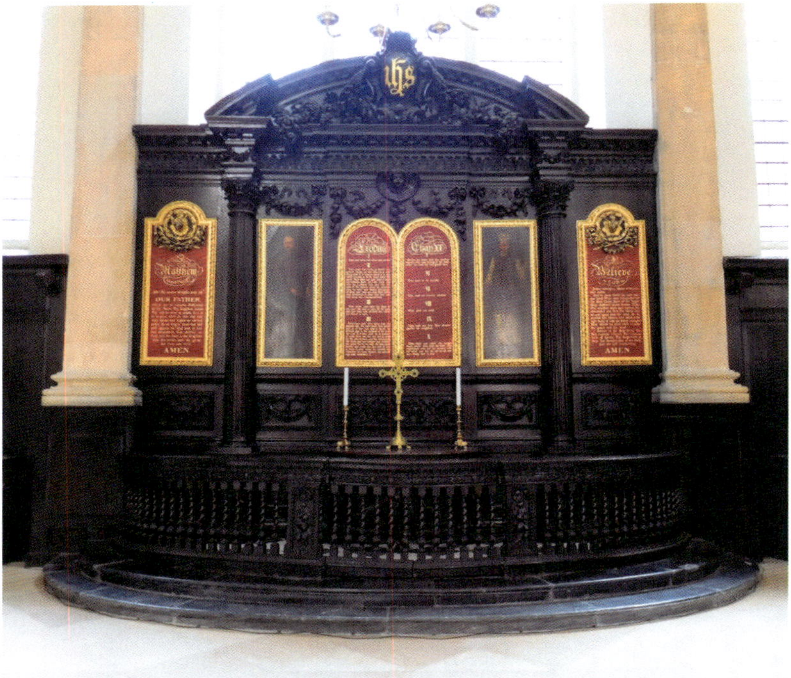
ihs
OUR FATHER
AMEN
AMEN

St. Stephen Walbrook

Location: 39 Walbrook, City
Closest Underground Stations: Bank, Cannon Street
Nearby Attractions: St. Paul's Cathedral, Leadenhall Market, Bank of England
Hours: 10am-4pm Mon.-Fri., closed Sat.-Sun., organ recital 12:30pm Fri.

THIS CHURCH WAS FOUNDED 1,000 YEARS AGO and has occupied the present site since 1428. The current building is by renowned architect Sir Christopher Wren and dates from 1672-1679. It is considered to be the masterpiece of Wren's city churches. Don't miss his magnificent dome, altar, pulpit and font. There also is a new altar in the center, starkly simple and massive in white stone, that was done in 1987 by Henry Moore.

One of the most memorable and poignant items is a simple old telephone in a glass case. This phone was used as the world's first "hotline" for despairing and suicidal people and the first of many thousands of emergency phones throughout the world. It is a tribute to one of the church's previous pastors, Chad Varah, who founded the Samaritans here in 1953.

[82]

Bankside Gallery

Location: 48 Hopton Street, Bankside
Closest Underground Stations: Blackfriars, Southwark
Nearby Attractions: Tate Modern, The Queen's Walk, Shakespeare's Globe
Hours: 11am-6pm daily
Admission: Free

FOR OVER 35 YEARS, THIS ART GALLERY HAS BEEN HOME TO TWO HISTORIC SOCIETIES, the Royal Watercolour Society and the Royal Society of Painter-Printmakers. It is located on the Queen's Walk on the south side of the Thames just to the right of the Tate Modern museum.

Here you will find changing exhibits of original prints and contemporary water-based works. Both established and new artists are represented, and many pieces are for sale. The gallery also supports art competitions and educational activities by members of the two societies. And there is a well-stocked bookshop with books on the theory and practice of watercolor and printmaking as well as a good collection of art history books.

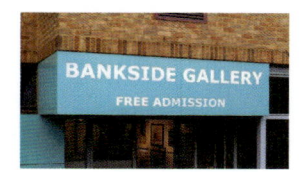

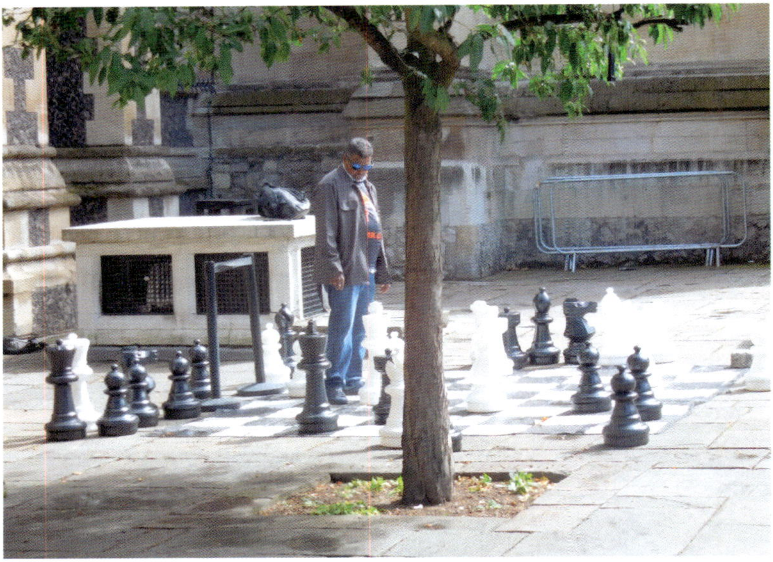

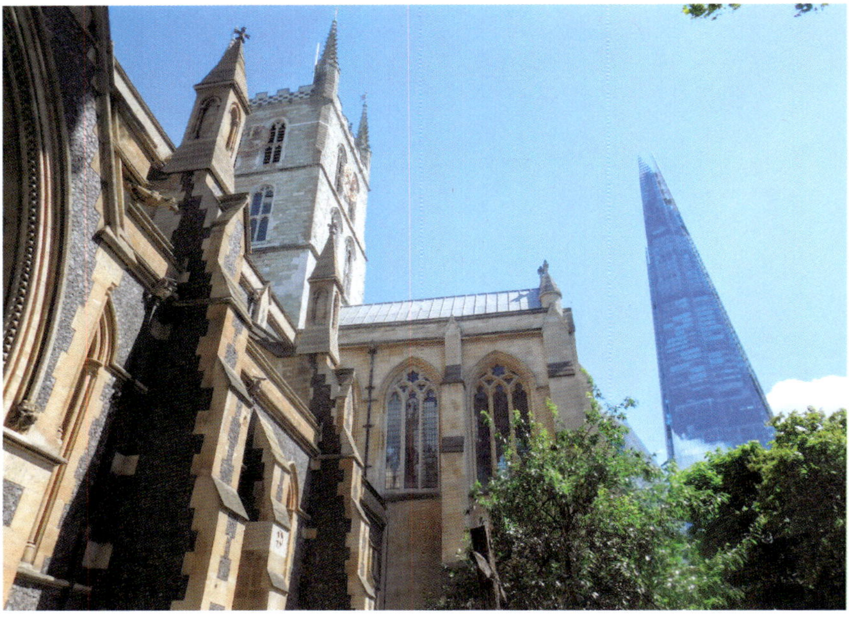

Millenium Courtyard of Southwark Cathedral

Location: Montague Close
Closest Underground Station: London Bridge
Nearby Attractions: Queen's Walk, Borough Market, Tower Bridge
Hours: 8:30 am to 6:00 pm

SITTING IN THE CLOISTER-STYLE COURTYARD, you are surrounded by lawns, benches, trees, shrubs and a giant chess set. Birds chirp and people talk in low voices. Looking up, you see the spire of a gigantic new glass building, the Shard, an interesting contrast to the architecture of the 15th century church.

The Southwark Cathedral is on the south bank of the Thames, close to London Bridge and Borough Market. For over 1,000 years, Christians have worshiped here—it was a convent in 606, a priory in 1106, a parish church in 1540 and a cathedral in 1905. It is the oldest Gothic church building in London and has some exquisite stained glass windows and a 13th century wooden effigy of a knight. One of the side chapels is dedicated to John Harvard, founder of Harvard University who was baptized here in 1607. William Shakespeare, Geoffrey Chaucer and Charles Dickens worshiped here, and it is believed that Shakespeare was present when John Harvard was baptized.

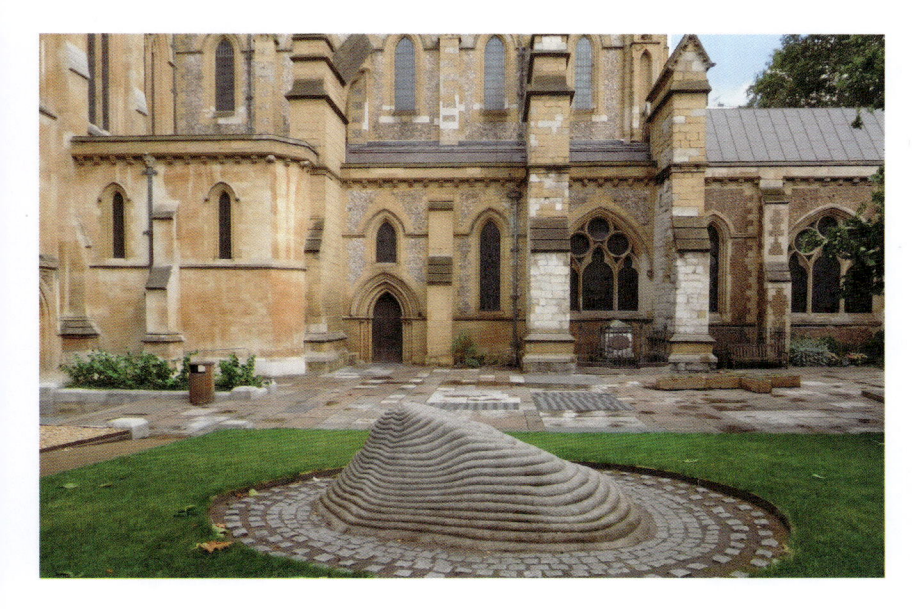

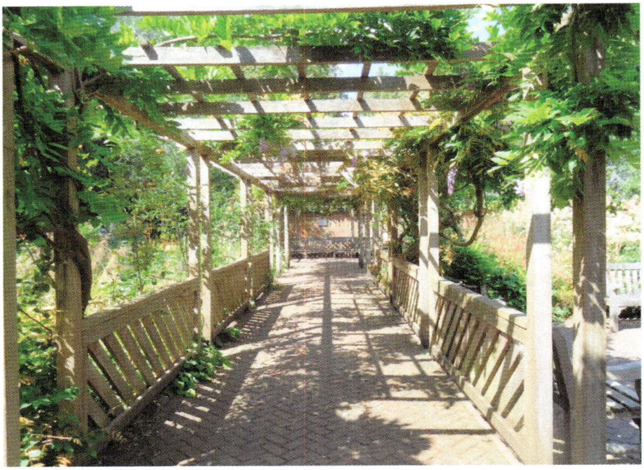

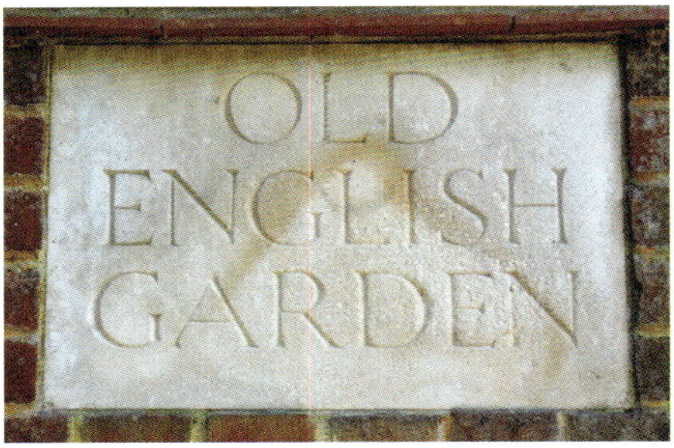
OLD
ENGLISH
GARDEN

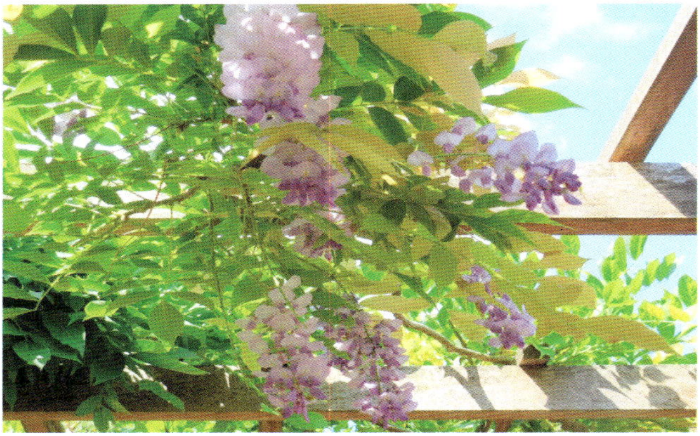

Old English Garden in Battersea Park

Location: In Battersea Park off Carriage Drive North, Chelsea
Closest Underground Station: Battersea
Nearby Attractions: Battersea Park, Royal Hospital of Chelsea, Chelsea Physic Garden
Hours: 6:30 am to 10:30 pm

BATTERSEA PARK IS A 250-ACRE GREENSPACE THAT OPENED IN 1858 on the south side of the Thames, across from the Chelsea Embankment. While not as centrally located as some of the other parks, it is among the most interesting and enjoyable.

An approach from the Chelsea Bridge in the east provides a great view of the park's major landmark, a Peace Pagoda which serves as a spiritual center for monks and followers from the Japanese Buddhist sect. On weekends, the park is full of people practicing yoga, riding bicycles, jogging, strolling with their children, picnicking, and napping on the lawns.

Wildlife here consists of ducks and birds including herons, cormorants and grebes living on or around the lake. There are over 4,000 trees from all over the world, some more than 150 years old. And there are at least nine different gardens, specializing in camellias, chrysanthemums, roses, vegetables and herbs. Conveniences include restrooms and snack bars.

Just off Carriage Drive North is one of the park's hidden secrets, the **Old English Garden**. Designated only by a small cement plaque on the brick wall, this quiet garden is hidden among the trees near the cricket pavilion and provides an oasis of calm in what can be a very busy park. It consists of a pool and fountain surrounded by a brick walkway, and a pergola covered with wisteria. Throughout the years, the Old English Garden has been a popular subject of London postcards.

Battersea Park is on the Register of Historic Parks and Gardens by English Heritage and should not be missed. For additional information about another special feature in the park, see *Festival Pleasure Gardens in Battersea Park*.

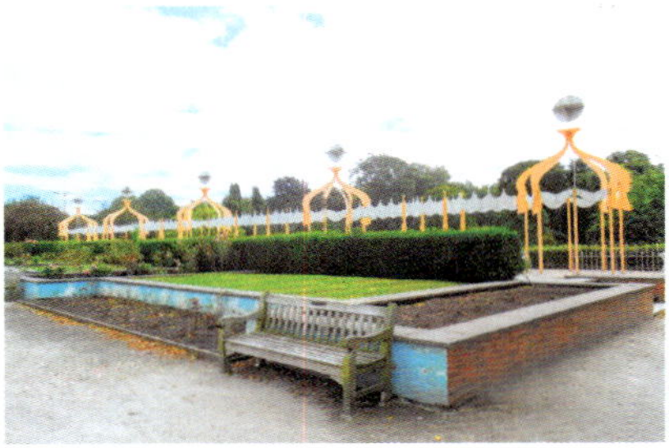

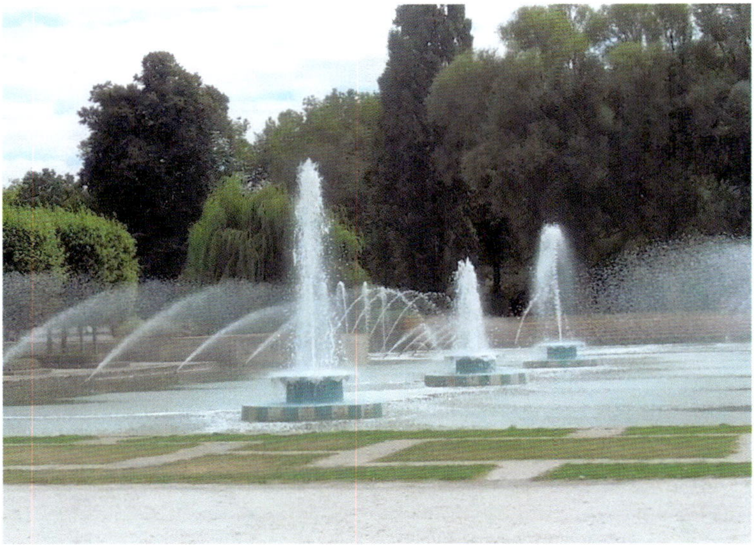

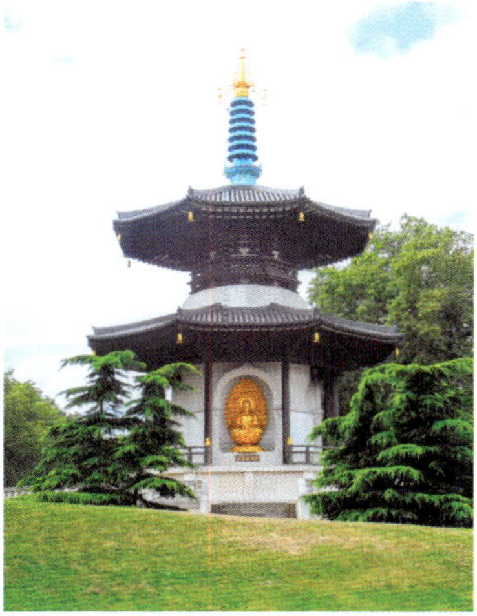

Festival Pleasure Gardens in Battersea Park

Location: In Battersea Park
Closest Underground Station: Battersea
Nearby Attractions: Battersea Park, Royal Hospital of Chelsea, Chelsea Physic Garden
Hours: 6:30 am to 10:30 pm

YOU CAN'T HELP BUT SMILE AS YOU ENCOUNTER THE FESTIVAL PLEASURE GARDENS in Battersea Park. In the midst of grassy hillocks filled with dazzling flower beds and set off by white benches is the centerpiece of the gardens, the spectacular fountains.

They were created for the 1951 Festival of Britain, an exhibition designed to give the public a feeling of recovery and renewal in the dismal days following the end of World War II. There were exhibitions throughout Britain celebrating its contribution to the arts, architecture, science, technology and industrial design, and forty acres of Battersea Park were given over to the gardens. Garden designer Russell Page worked alongside a theatrical designer and an artist to create this magical site for the Festival.

Many of the original structures have deteriorated or were demolished in the years following the Festival, but what remains today are magnificent and enjoyed by all—the flower gardens, the fountain displays and a tea terrace with a fanciful pergola.

For additional information about Battersea Park and its other special features, see *Old English Garden in Battersea Park.*

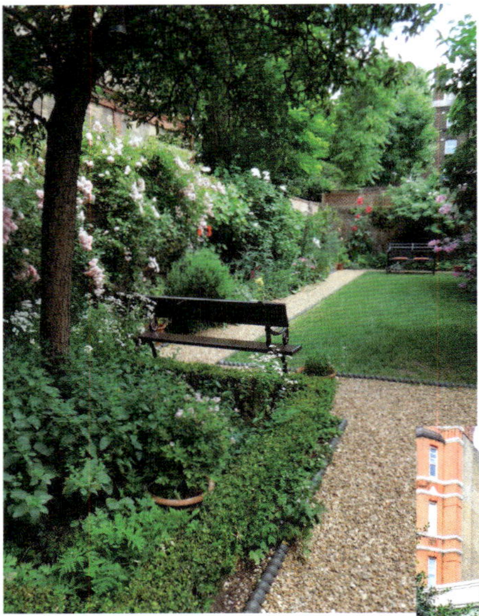

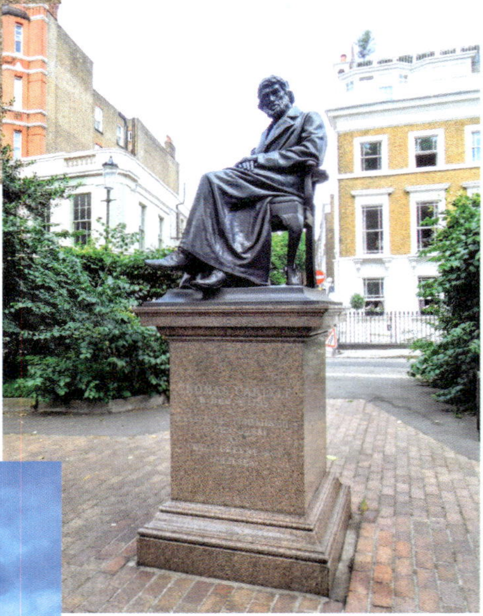

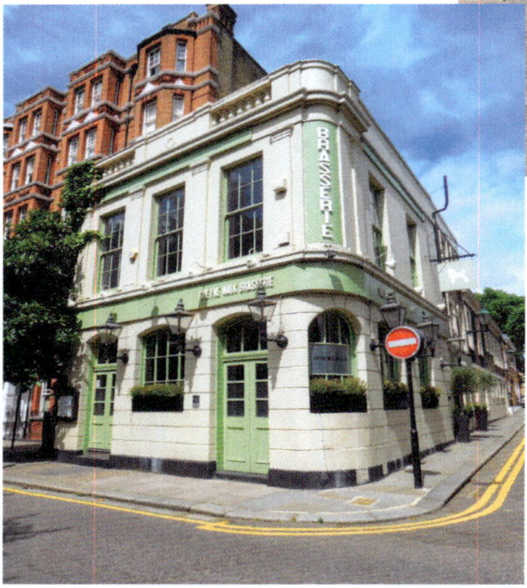
BRASSERIE

Carlyle's House

Location: 24 Cheyne Row, Chelsea
Closest Underground Stations: Sloane Square, South Kensington
Nearby Attractions: Chelsea Physic Garden, Battersea Park, Chelsea Royal Hospital
Hours: 11am-5pm Wed.-Sun., closed Mon.-Tues.

THOMAS CARLYLE (1795-1881), HISTORIAN, PHILOSOPHER, WRITER, AND FOUNDER of the London Library lived here (some say platonically) with his wife Jane Welsh Carlyle who was a woman of letters. Carlyle was a prolific writer yet few people have read his works because they are difficult to read, have been superseded by more contemporary writings, and are considered politically incorrect in today's world. His most notable works are *The French Revolution* and *On Heroes, Hero Worship, and The Heroic in History*.

The house in which the Carlyles lived was built in 1708 and is set up as it was when they lived here. This was *the* place to visit in the 19th century literary and intellectual worlds. Dickens, Darwin, Tennyson and other notables were regular guests here. Chelsea was not an upscale part of town at the time, and this is considered to be a modest house. You can tour the kitchen, the parlor, the drawing room/library, Jane's bedroom, and the study in the attic where Thomas did most of his writing.

There also is a restful garden out back—narrow, rectangular and enclosed by high brick walls as is typical of London gardens. It too is laid out much as it was when the Carlyles lived here and grew flowers, herbs and vegetables. There are benches, stone paths and plantings of boxwood, fruit trees, grapevines and roses.

Cheyne Walk is just a few steps down the street and there on the corner you will find the pretty green and white Cheyne Walk Brasserie where you can grab a bite to eat. Also on Cheyne Walk are some stunning old buildings and a magnificent statue of Thomas Carlyle.

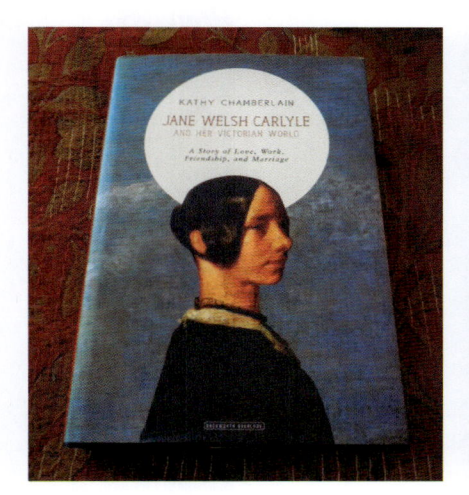

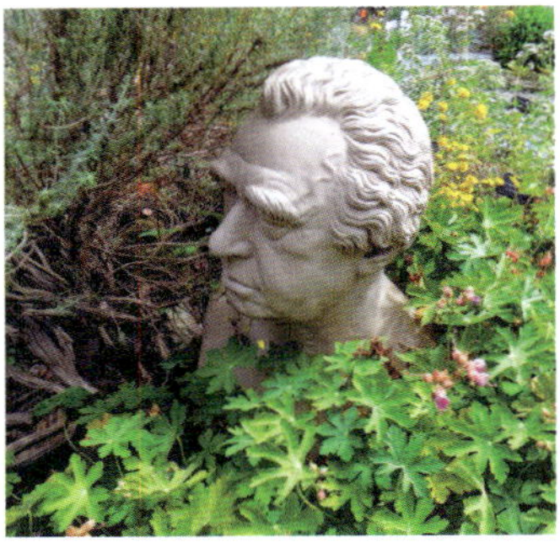

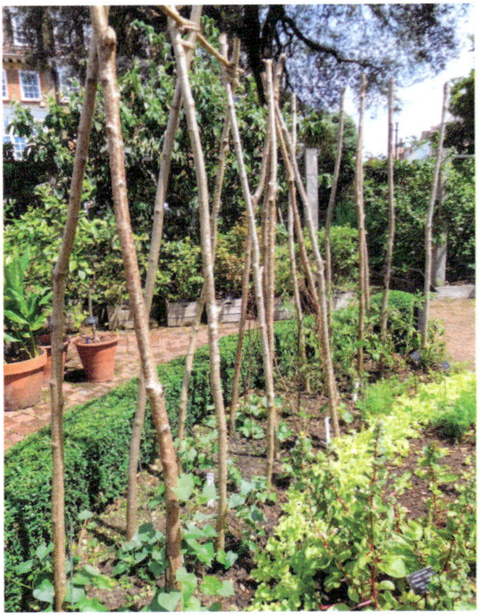

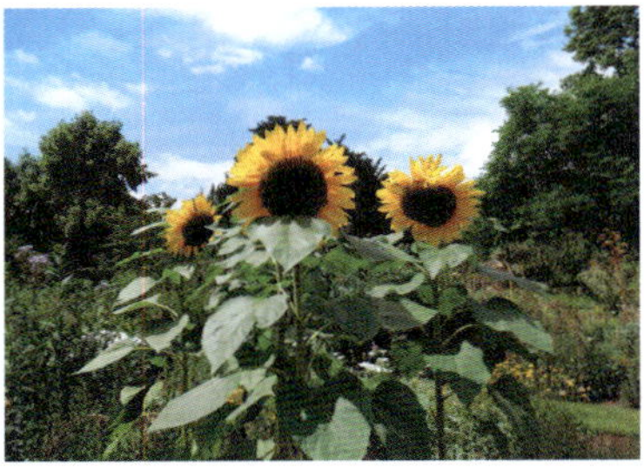

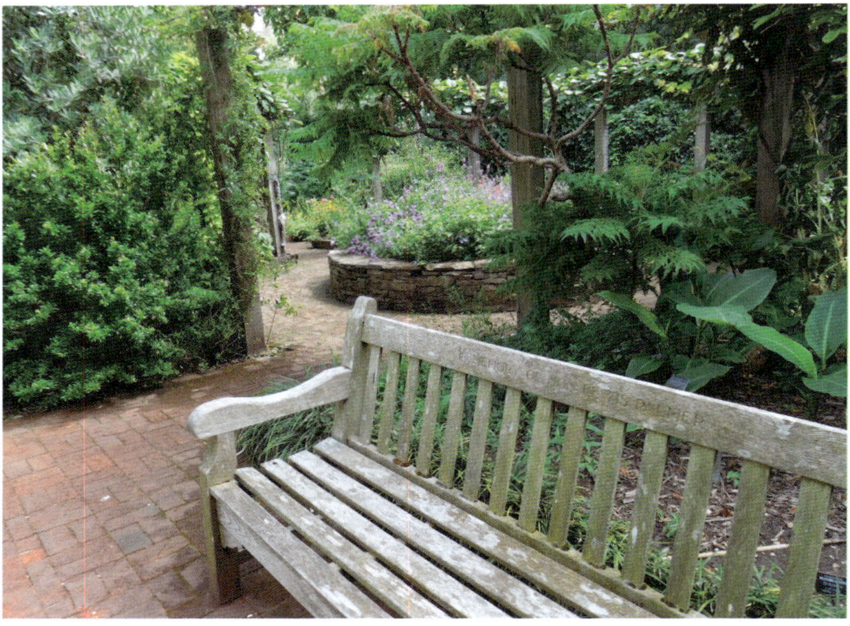

Chelsea Physic Garden

Location: 66 Royal Hospital Road, entrance on Swan Walk
Closest Underground Station: Sloane Square
Nearby Attractions: Chelsea Royal Hospital, Battersea Park, Carlyle's House
Hours: 11am-6pm Sun.-Fri., closed Sat.

According to a sign in this small walled garden, "[e]ighty percent of the world's population relies mainly on herbal medicine as their source of primary health care because it is cheap, easily accessible and traditional." This is a doctor's botanical garden and it sits on three and a half acres in a quiet residential area near the Thames not far from the congestion of busy Chelsea. It dates from 1673 and is the most richly stocked in the world.

The garden was a gift from Sir Hans Sloane, a physician who also studied botany and was very particular about classifying and labeling plant material. In 1713, he bought a manor that included the Chelsea Physic Garden where he had studied as a youth, and donated it to the Company of Apothecaries. As a token of their appreciation, the Company commissioned a statue of him, a copy of which still stands in the center of the garden.

This is an immaculate, peaceful and lovely place to take a stroll along the brick pathways that define areas by specialty. Specimens are meticulously labeled and there are signs that describe treatments using the plant material. There are plenty of benches where you can sit to ponder your ailments and how they could be treated with herbs. Be sure not to miss the olive tree, unusual for this climate, and the rock garden with its alpine plants.

Free tours of the gardens are offered, or you can pick up a map and audio guide and do it yourself (this is not well promoted, but it comes with your admission ticket so be sure to ask for it). They also run workshops, offer family activities, and have a highly-rated cafe where you can enjoy fresh and healthy foods.

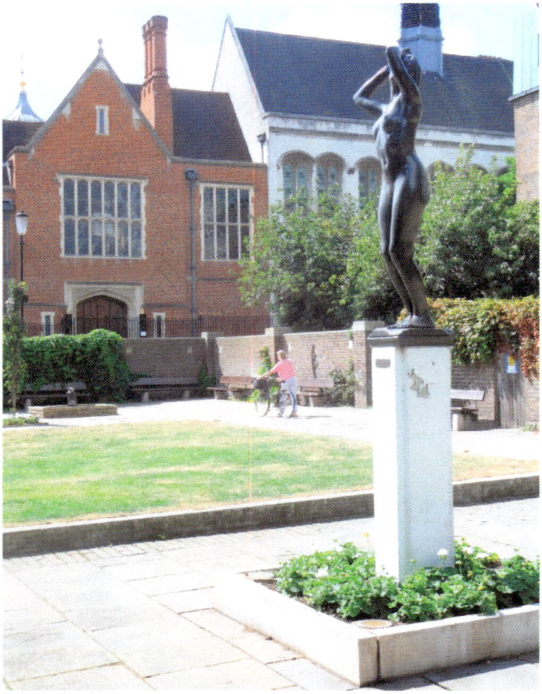

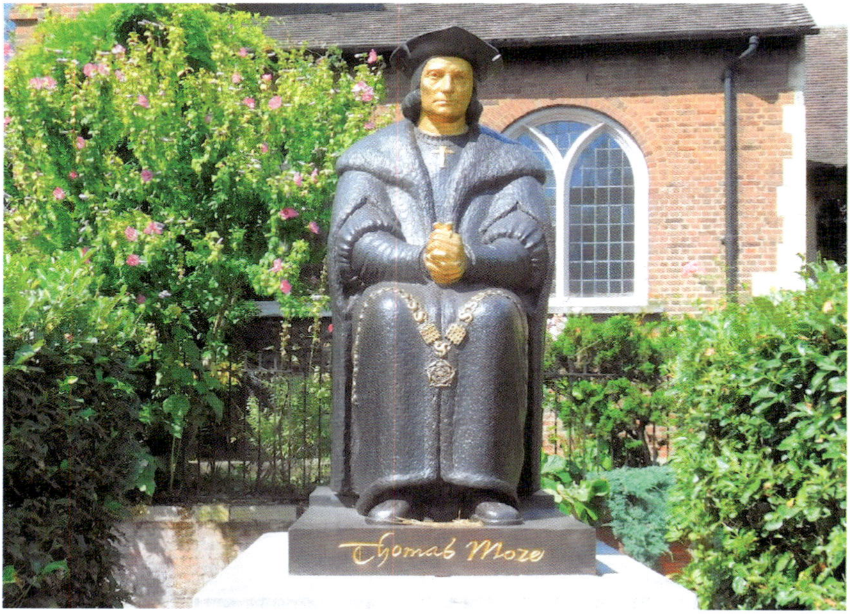
Thomas More

Roper's Garden

Location: Cheyne Walk, Chelsea, facing the River Thames
Closest Underground Station: Sloane Square
Nearby Attractions: Battersea Park, Carlyle's House, Chelsea Physic Garden

LOCATED IN THE BOROUGH OF CHELSEA, THIS TINY SUNKEN GARDEN ON TWO LEVELS is only about one-third of an acre. It was constructed in 1964 on the site of buildings destroyed by mines during World War II and consists of two benches, some sheltered seating, flowering shrubs and lawns. Overlooking the garden is Crosby Hall, part of a lovely 1466 mansion that belonged to Richard III and is now in private hands.

Prominent in the center of the garden is a statue of an ideal nude entitled *Awakening* by Gilbert Ledward. It dates from 1923. In the sunken garden is a stone panel of another nude. This one is entitled *Woman Taking Off Her Dress* and is quite the opposite of the ideal figure of *Awakening*; she is headless and rotund. Created in 1950 by Jacob Epstein, it is known as *Epstein's Nude* and is not very popular among locals.

The site of the garden was part of a wedding gift given by Sir Thomas More, author, philosopher, journalist, lawyer and saint, to his daughter Margaret who married William Roper in 1521. Not far from the garden, also on the Chelsea Embankment and Cheyne Walk, is a stunning painted statue of Sir Thomas More with hands clenched tightly in prayer.

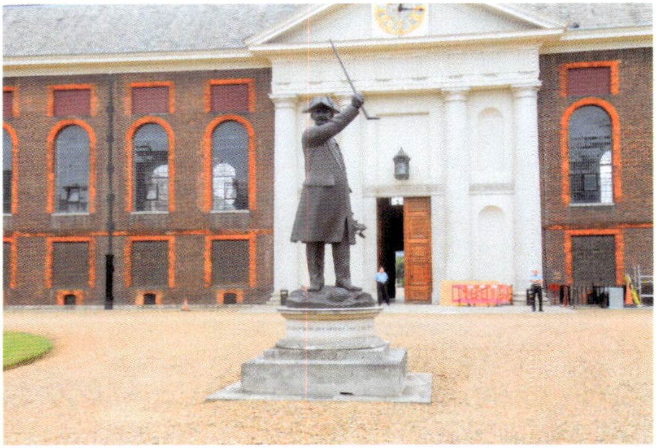

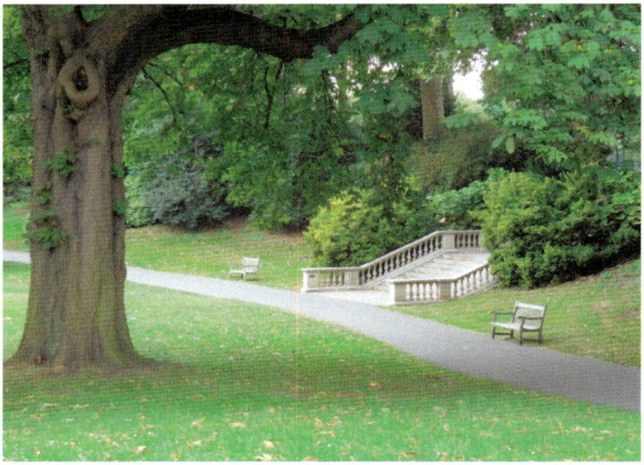

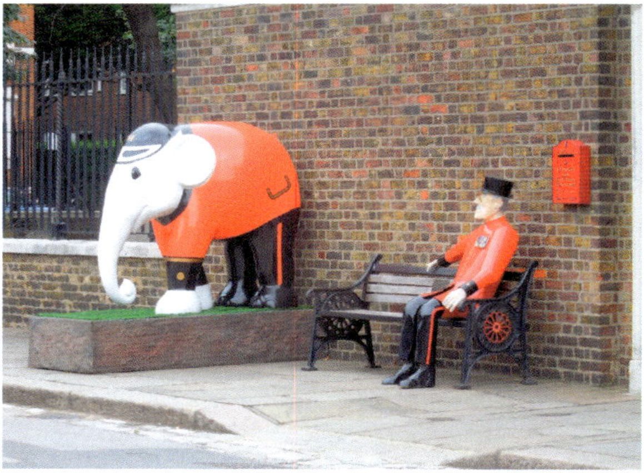

Old Burial Ground, Royal Hospital of Chelsea

Location: Royal Hospital Road, Chelsea
Closest Underground Station: Sloane Square
Nearby Attractions: Battersea Park, Chelsea Physic Garden
Admission: Free

THE OLD BURIAL GROUND IS WITHIN THE COMPLEX OF THE ROYAL HOSPITAL of Chelsea, Home of the Chelsea Pensioners. In-pensioners were buried here between 1692 and 1854, when other options were made available, and in 2004, the burial ground was re-opened for the interment of cremated remains only. Take a seat and contemplate the lives of those who rest here in eternity.

The **Royal Hospital** was designed by Christopher Wren and completed in 1692. It is a retirement and nursing home for old and wounded soldiers of the British Army known as "pensioners" and today, about 320 army veterans are spending their later years in this very special place. On the grounds are a breathtaking and opulent chapel designed by Wren, state apartments that were built to host members of the Royal Family, a lovely central courtyard with a gilded statue of Charles II, a museum and a gift shop. Nearby are the secluded Ranelagh Gardens with their winding walkways and statues, and a lovely Italian staircase climbing up a hillside, seemingly going nowhere.

You can book a tour of the Royal Hospital on its website, led by one of the iconic Chelsea Pensioners in full uniform.

[98]

Saatchi Gallery

Location: Duke of York's HQ, King's Road, Chelsea
Closest Underground Station: Sloane Square
Nearby Attractions: Royal Hospital, Chelsea Physic Garden, Cheyne Walk
Hours: 10am-6pm daily
Admission: Free

THIS ART GALLERY IN CHELSEA PROVIDES A FORUM FOR CONTEMPORARY ARTISTS to express themselves, especially those largely unknown young artists and those international artists who have not exhibited in the UK. It opened more than 25 years ago, and moved to its current location in the historic Duke of York's headquarters building in 2008.

This is a place where you will find simple presentations in large open rooms that are exciting, thought-provoking, touching and unconventional. All are presented aesthetically and some of the more provocative exhibits can be highly emotional and not suitable to all audiences. Photography, painting, sculpture and other media are represented.

An example of the type of exhibit you will find here is the *From Selfies to Self-Expression* exhibit in the summer of 2017. This was a captivating, quirky and provocative study of the era of the selfie. It started with a historical display of classic self portraits done by famous artists, then went on to contemporary selfies that at times were shocking and highly emotional, celebrity selfies, and an interactive exhibit where you could photograph yourself taking a selfie with white smoke billowing from your eyes.

The gallery's Mess provides sophisticated comfort food using fresh ingredients. There also are charming cafes along King's Road where you can grab a bite to eat. One is the Oree boulangerie and patisserie at 65 King's Road that serves wonderful French cafe foods made fresh daily.

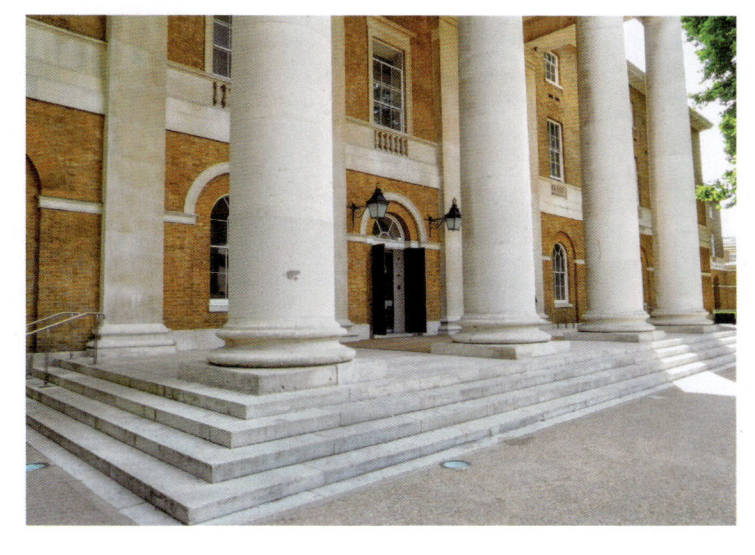

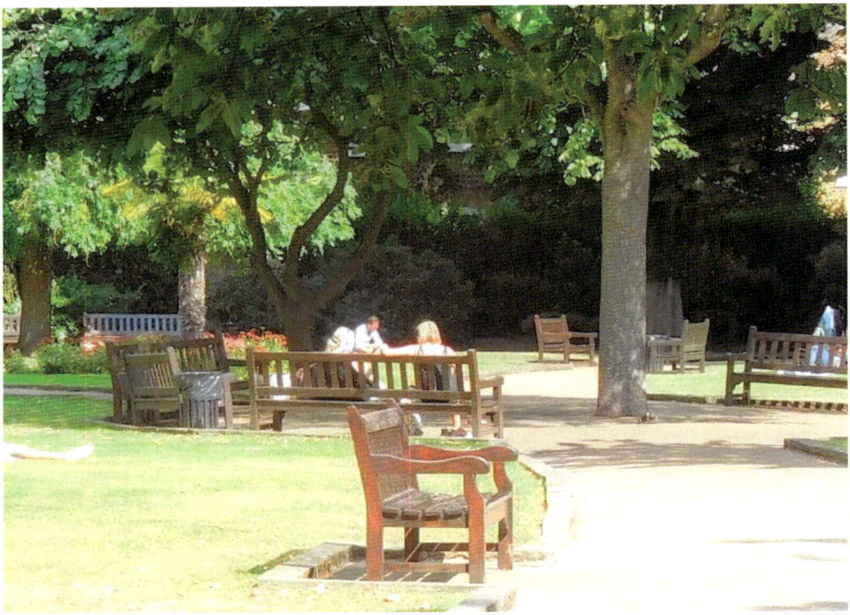

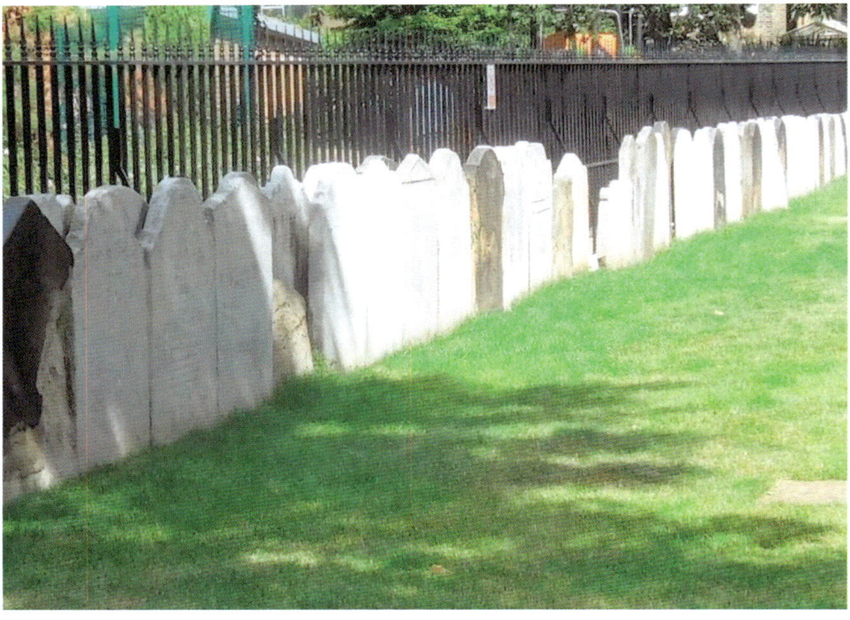

Gardens of the Parish Church of St. Luke

Location: Sydney Street, Chelsea
Closest Underground Stations: South Kensington, Sloane Square
Nearby Attractions: Royal Hospital of the Chelsea Pensioners

Nestled on a side street away from the hustle and bustle of King's Road in Chelsea is the serene churchyard of the Parish Church of St. Luke. Flower beds, old London plane trees, sprawling lawns and plenty of benches are features that weary tourists can enjoy. The churchyard is a former burial ground that was converted into a public garden in 1881. The old gravestones, memorials to locals and parishioners, were removed and placed around the perimeter of the church to form a boundary wall.

The church itself was built in 1820 and is one of the first neo-Gothic churches in London. It is a handsome building that resembles King's College Chapel in Cambridge, England. Charles Dickens was married here in 1835, two days after the first part of the *Pickwick Papers* was published. Inside the church building is Café Portico, open from 9:30 am to 4 pm for breakfast, lunch and afternoon tea.

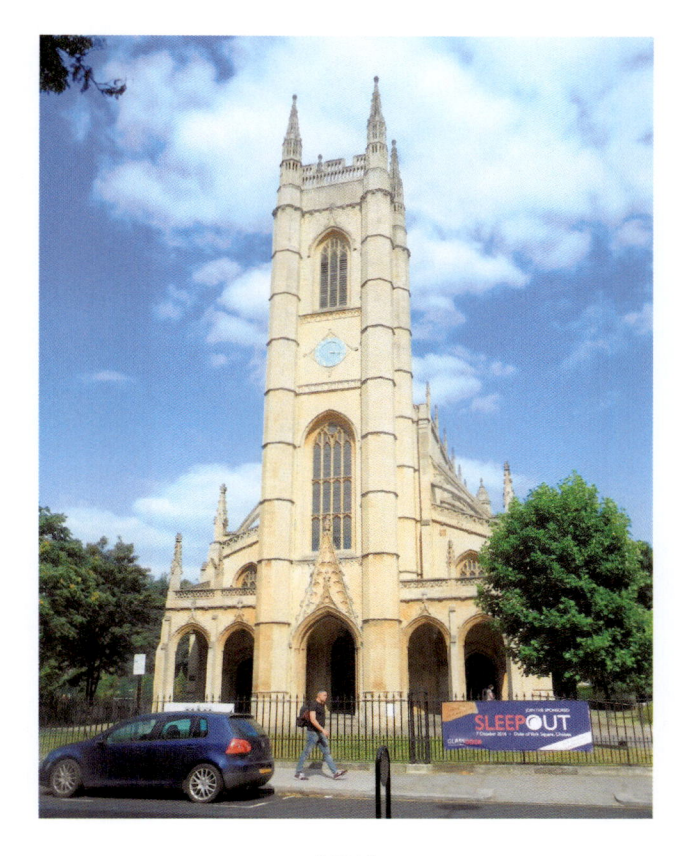

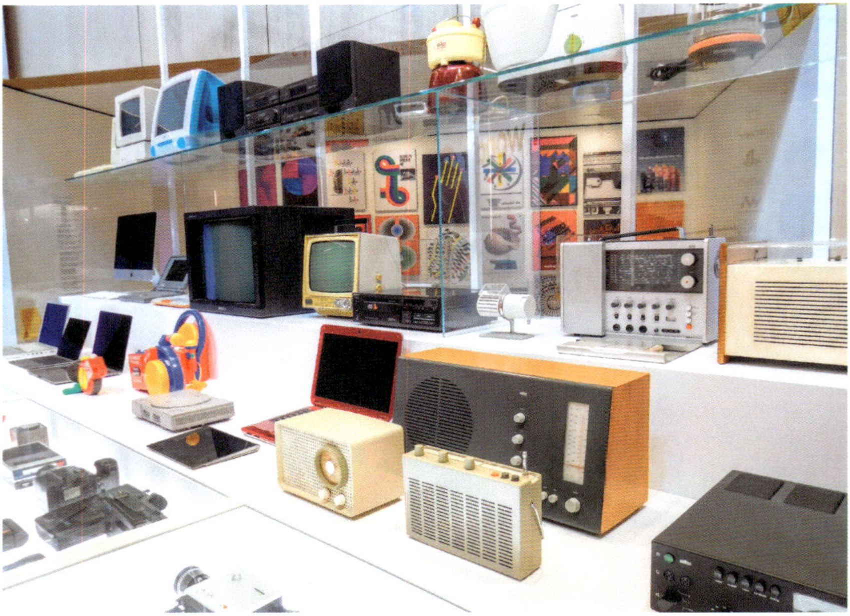

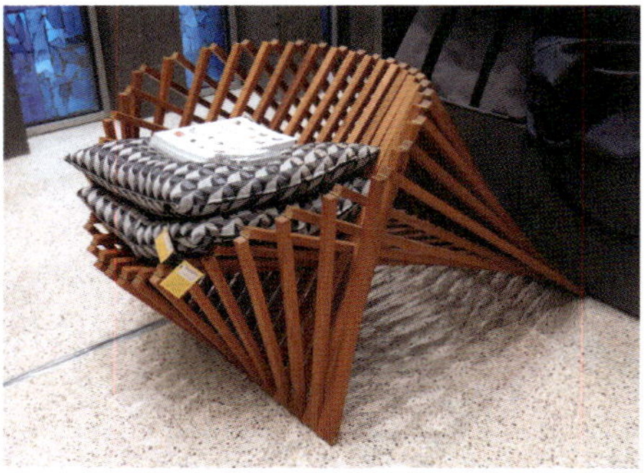

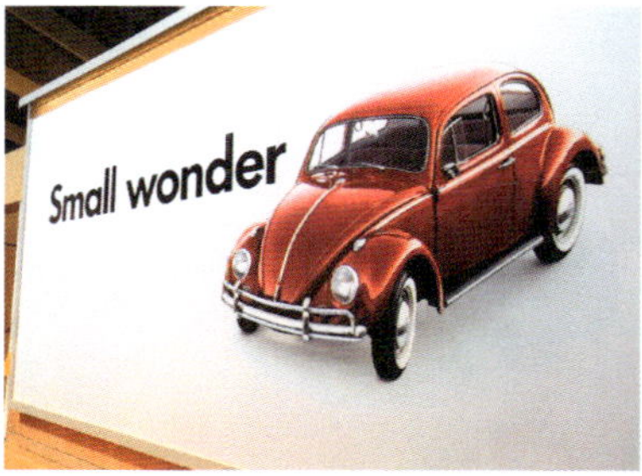
Small wonder

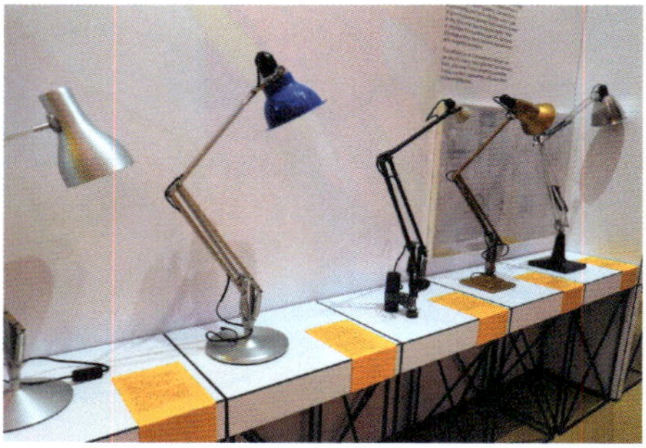

Design Museum

Location: 224-238 High Street Kensington
Closest Underground Station: High Street Kensington
Nearby attractions: Kensington Roof Gardens, Holland Park
Hours: 10am-5:45pm daily
Admission: Free for the permanent collection; charge for special exhibits

THIS INTERESTING MUSEUM WAS FOUNDED IN 1989 and showcases all elements of design, including architecture, fashion, products, and industrial and graphic design. Here you can admire the designs of contemporary shoes, the bentwood chair, the Volkswagen Beetle, and the map of the Underground, and see how designs have evolved over the years in chairs, television sets, radios and computers. There is something here for everyone.

The building itself is architecturally stunning. Built in the 1960s, it was restored in 2011-2016 to accommodate the needs of a modern museum. Temporary and permanent exhibits, some interactive, are displayed over several levels.

Designer-Maker-User is a permanent exhibit of key objects from the museum's collection. It explores design from the perspective of all three and shows how the designer is influenced by the needs and wants of the users, how the users adopt the designs created, and how technology affects the work of the makers.

The museum presents annual awards for *Design of the Year* in several categories, has a Designer in Residence program, and offers workshops and lectures. There also is a reference library, gift shop and cafe.

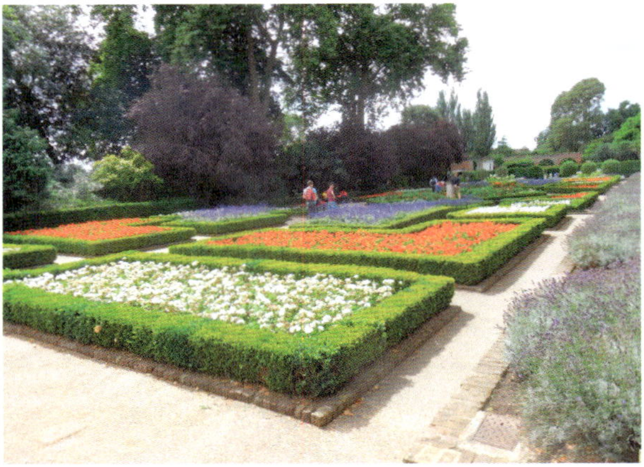

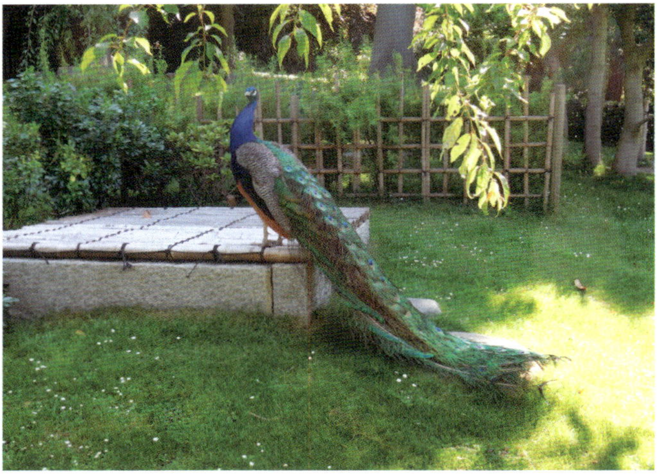

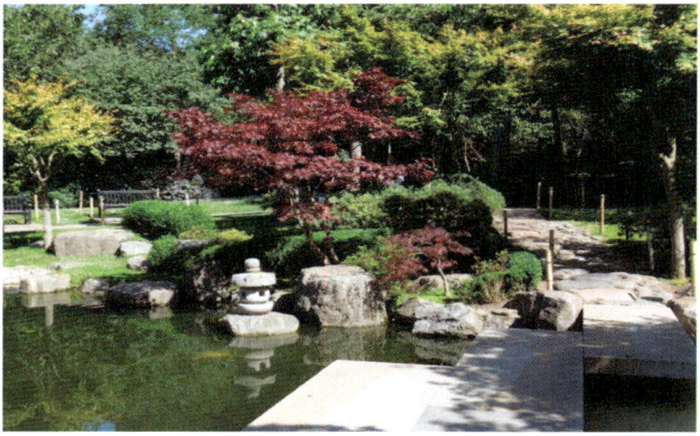

Japanese and Dutch Gardens in Holland Park

Location: Abbotsbury Road and Holland Walk
Closest Underground Stations: Holland Park, High Street Kensington
Nearby attractions: Kensington Palace, Kensington Gardens, Notting Hill, Design Museum
Hours: Mon-Sun 7:30 am to 6:00 pm, subject to change

HOLLAND PARK IS A LOVELY 54-ACRE PARK IN AN ELITE SECTION OF LONDON, a few blocks west of Kensington Palace and Gardens. The park opened in 1952 on what remained of the grounds of Holland House, a Jacobean mansion dating from the 17th century which had been largely demolished. Stunning Victorian houses and terraces line the streets in this area, and shops, cafes and restaurants cater to an affluent clientele.

The northern half of the park is mainly woodland abundant with wildlife, including some resident peacocks, and the southern part includes a ball park and is used for sports and recreation. In the central section surrounding the ruins of Holland House are the Japanese and Dutch Gardens. This is a more formal area and, besides the gardens, includes an orangery now used as an exhibition space and a restaurant where the old ice house and ballroom were located.

The **Dutch garden** was laid out in the 19th century when Holland House was in its heyday as a gathering place for socialites, artists, writers and politicians. It contains formal beds of colorful plantings, stunning displays of roses, water features and some modern sculpture.

The **Kyoto Garden** was donated by the Kyoto Chamber of Commerce for the 1991 London Festival of Japan. It is a magnificent space containing all the elements of a Japanese garden—water, rocks, a bridge, stone lanterns, trees, flowers and fish. Children holding their parents' hands walk along the stone walkway over the pond, listening to the waterfall up above and fascinated by the koi down below.

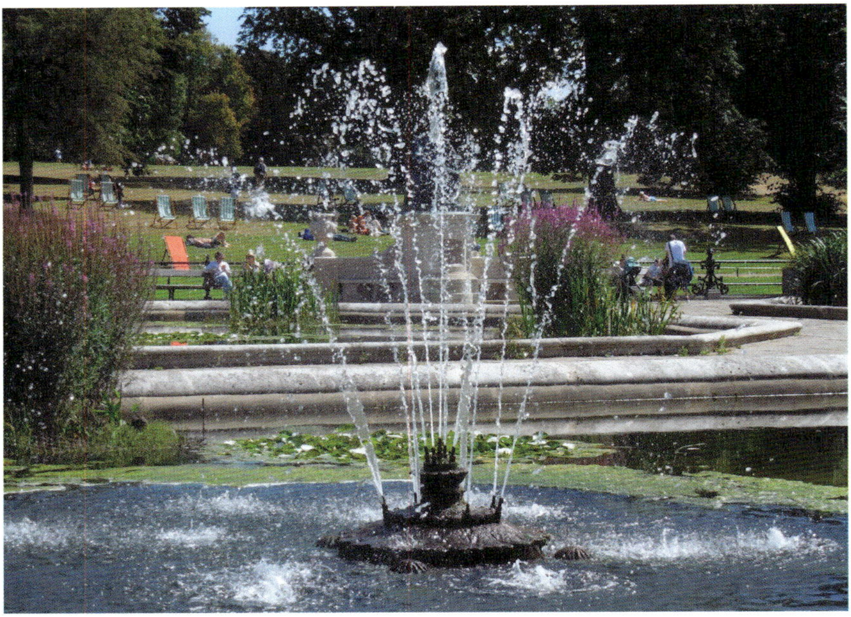

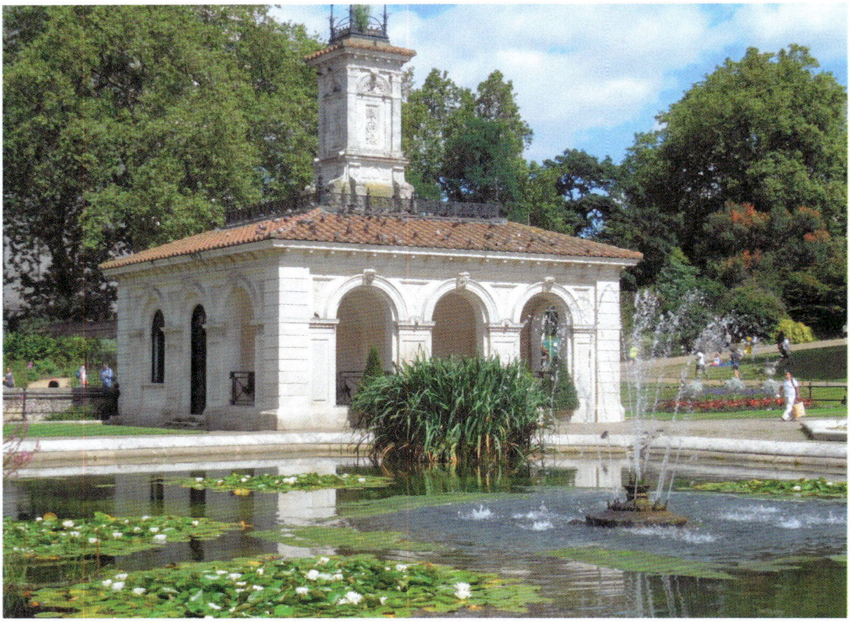

Italian Garden in Kensington Gardens

Location: Kensington Gardens near Lancaster Gate
Closest Underground Station: Lancaster Gate
Nearby Attractions: Kensington Gardens, Hyde Park

Kensington Gardens have a lot to offer—Kensington Palace, the royal palace overlooking Round Pond; the Diana Memorial Playground that delights a million children every year; a charming statue of Peter Pan nestled in the shrubs near the river; the Albert Memorial commemorating Prince Albert's death from typhoid in 1861; the Serpentine Galleries; and the elegant Italian Garden.

The Italian Garden is a 150-year-old ornamental water garden located near Lancaster Gate and overlooking The Long Water, a river that flows into the Serpentine in nearby Hyde Park. It is believed to have been a gift from Prince Albert to his adored Queen Victoria. Within the gardens you will find splendid geometric flower beds, four basins made of Carrera marble with fountains in the middle, decorative stone urns, terraces, and a beautiful pump house where you can see Queen Victoria and Prince Albert's initials on one of the walls. The famous Tazza fountain stands at the head of The Long Water and is known for the mermen that support the bowl.

These gardens were built in 1860 and restored in 2011 using a grant from the Tiffany & Co. Foundation. They are listed by English Heritage as a site of distinct importance.

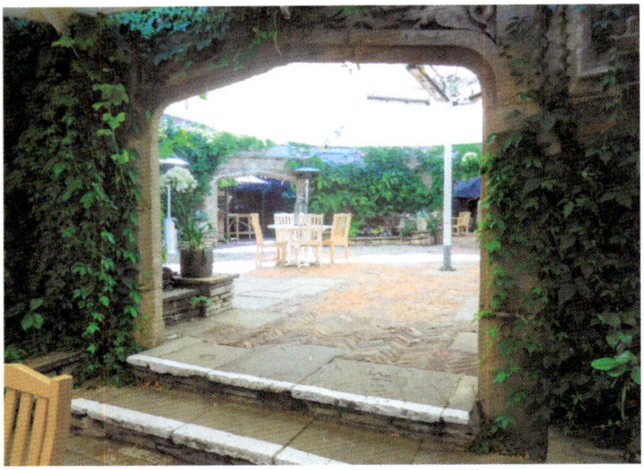

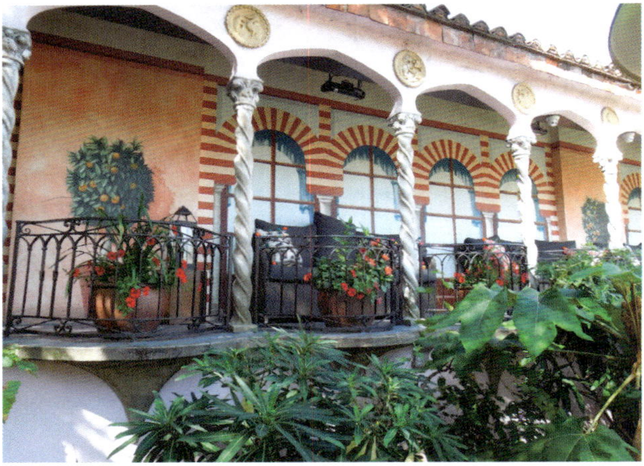

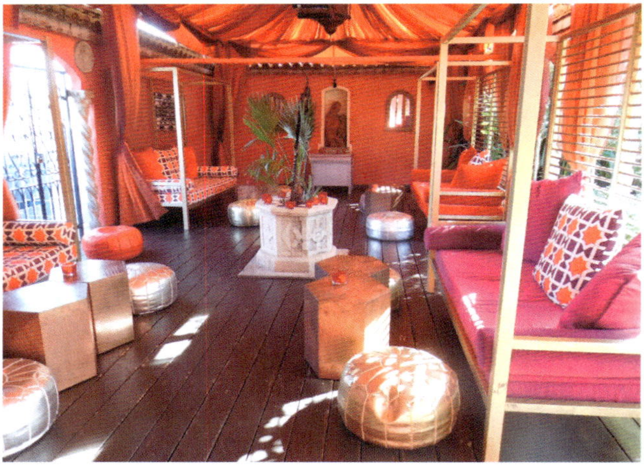

Kensington Roof Gardens

Location: 99 Kensington High Street, entrance on Derry Street
Closest Underground Station: High Street Kensington
Nearby Attractions: Holland Park, Kensington Palace, Kensington Gardens
Website: www.virginlimitededition.com/en/the-roof-gardens/the-gardens
Phone: 020 7937 7994
Admission: Free

This place is phenomenol and unique. Created in the 1930s on the 6th floor rooftop over Derry & Toms department store, now home to a number of smaller stores, the roof gardens consist of three lovely themed gardens on one and a half acres. The Spanish garden is small and formal and reminiscent of Spain's Alhambra. It has colorful tiles, painted arches, wicker sofas and chairs, throw pillows, palm trees, a Moorish sun pavilion and panoramic views over London's skyline. The brick-walled Tudor garden is made up of three courtyards and vine-covered Tudor-style archways and is suitable for wedding and other celebrations. And the English woodland garden has a big variety of trees, a running brook, a giant chess set and a pond stocked with fish. There are over 70 full-size trees up here, ducks paddle in the brook, and four resident pink flamingos show off on one leg in the pool of water at the beginning of the stream.

Kensington Roof Gardens is a spectacular and extraordinary landmark that has won many awards over the years and you should not miss it. It is an event venue so you have to plan your visit according to their schedule. Check their website, which they update weekly, and call before you go. The small effort is well worth it.

[110]

Leighton House Museum and Art Gallery

Location: 12 Holland Park Road
Closest Underground Station: High Street Kensington
Nearby Attractions: Holland Park, Kensington Roof Gardens, Design Museum
Hours: 10am-5:30pm Wed.-Mon., closed Tues.

FREDERIC LORD LEIGHTON (1830-1896), A MAJOR VICTORIAN PAINTER AND SCULPTOR, lived and worked in this simple brick building in the elegant neighborhood surrounding Holland Park. The house was custom built by Lord Leighton in the 1860s and, although it is simple on the outside, on the inside he transformed it into his own "private palace of art".

The Arab Hall is the focal point of the house. It is an exquisite fantasy with marble pillars, 16th and 17th mosaic wall panels, and floors in blue tiles from Syria, Turkey and Iran. The pool with a small fountain in the center of the room provides an air of calm. And over it all is a spectacular domed ceiling covered in gold leaf.

Leighton was a prolific artist and sculptor. Upstairs you will find his work and some personal objects as well as works by some of his contemporaries.

This house-museum gives an insight into the lives of artists of this period. For a richer experience, take the tour offered by the curator. Unfortunately, photos are not allowed inside the house.

After touring Leighton House, stop by the Primrose Bakery on the corner of Melbury Road and Kensington High Street for a cup of tea and one of their signature cupcakes.

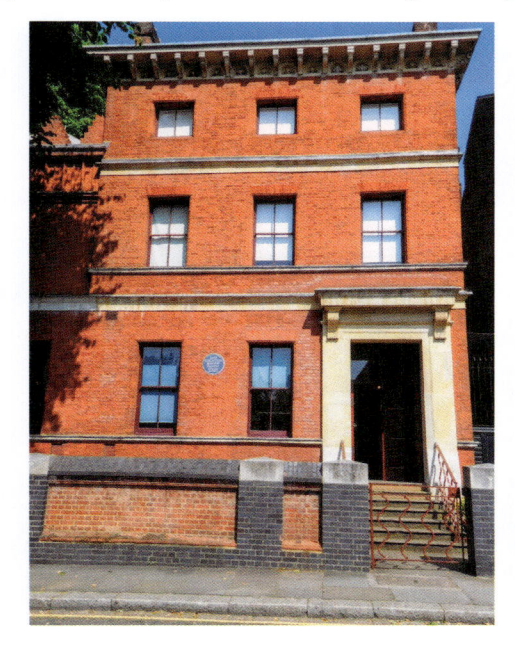

[112]

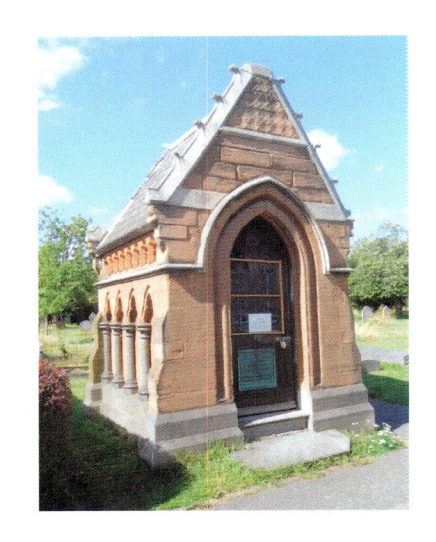

Margravine Cemetery

Location: West Kensington, Hammersmith
Closest Underground Stations: Baron's Court, West Kensington

I HAPPENED UPON THIS SERENE PLACE when I was strolling the West Kensington area. Originally the land now occupied by the cemetery was used for gardens and orchards. That was when burials took place in graveyards associated with churches. Then, in 1869 this land was converted into a cemetery because church graveyards had become overcrowded, made even more urgent by outbreaks of cholera. Over the next 80 or so years, more than 80,000 burials took place in Margravine Cemetery.

During World War II, bombs damaged many of the gravestones. After the war ended, the process of burying many of the headstones was begun, some of the area was grassed over, and the cemetery was transformed into a "garden of rest". Today it forms part of a conservation area and includes trees and grassland rich in wildflowers and a wide variety of birds. Very few burials take place now, and then only in privately-owned graves. The headstones that remain are old and lovely, some tilting precariously and others in damaged condition, but they are beautiful memorials to the past. A few are lovingly cared for by family members, but most remain neglected and overgrown.

It is very peaceful wandering the paths of Margravine Cemetery. The walkways are mostly deserted, you can hear the birds chirping, and you're likely to encounter only one or two other souls resting on benches, walking their dogs, or reading a book as they lean against a crumbling headstone.

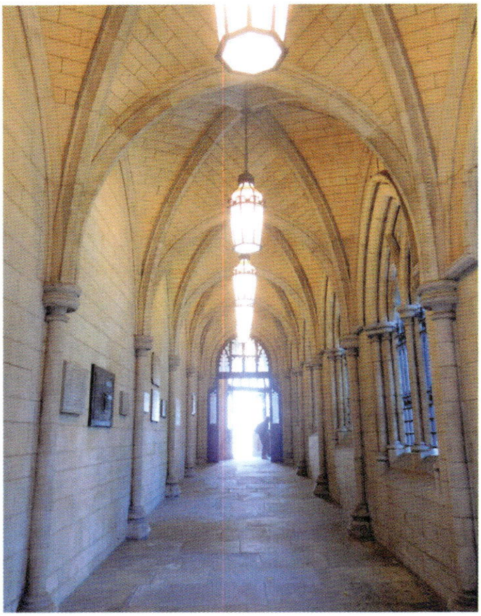

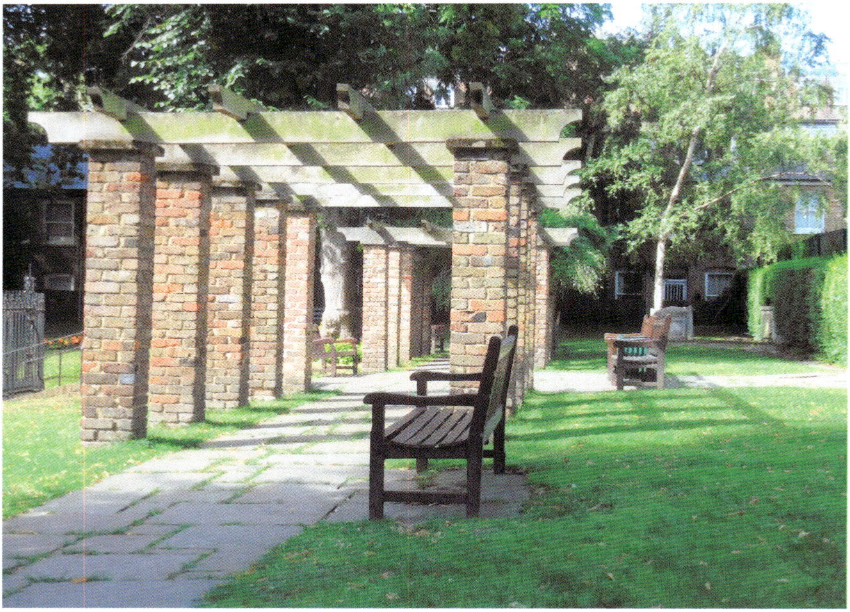

St. Mary Abbots Schoolyard and Alleyway

Location: Corner of Kensington High Street and Vicarage Street
Closest Underground Station: Kensington High Street
Nearby Attractions: Kensington Palace, Kensington Gardens, Kensington Roof Gardens

ST. MARY ABBOTS IS "WHERE BABIES ARE BAPTISED, lovers wed and those who have died are laid to rest". The entrance to the church and schoolyard is off Kensington High Street and is quite stunning with its long arched hallway adorned with chandeliers and funerary monuments from the 17th century. Parishioners of St. Mary Abbots included Sir Isaac Newton and author Beatrix Potter.

The associated primary school was founded in 1707 as a charity school, but the buildings in the schoolyard are later, dating from 1875. Noteworthy are the charming painted statues of a boy and a girl and the inscribed stone doorways, one for *Boys & Infants* and another for *Girls*. Take a moment and relax under the pergola and shade trees.

Church Walk is a charming quiet alley off the courtyard with an odd assortment of tiny shops. There's a milliner, a hairdresser, a skin care salon, a knife store, and a men's clothier.

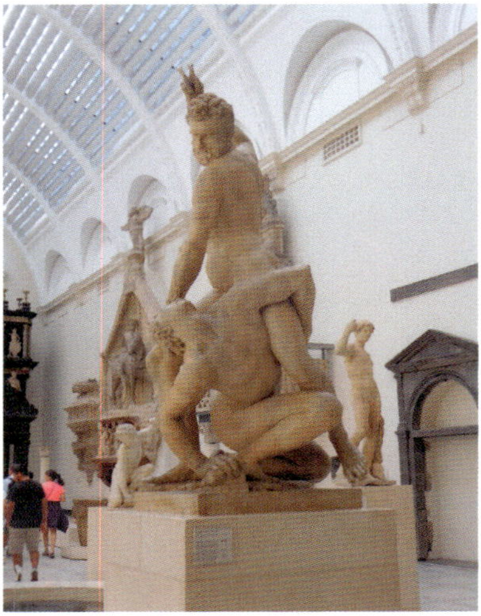

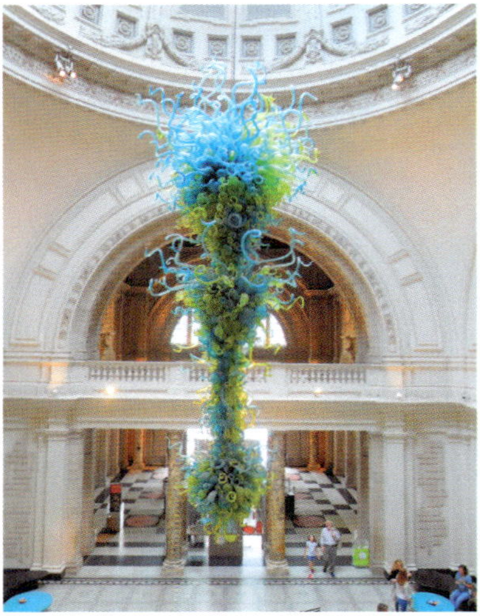

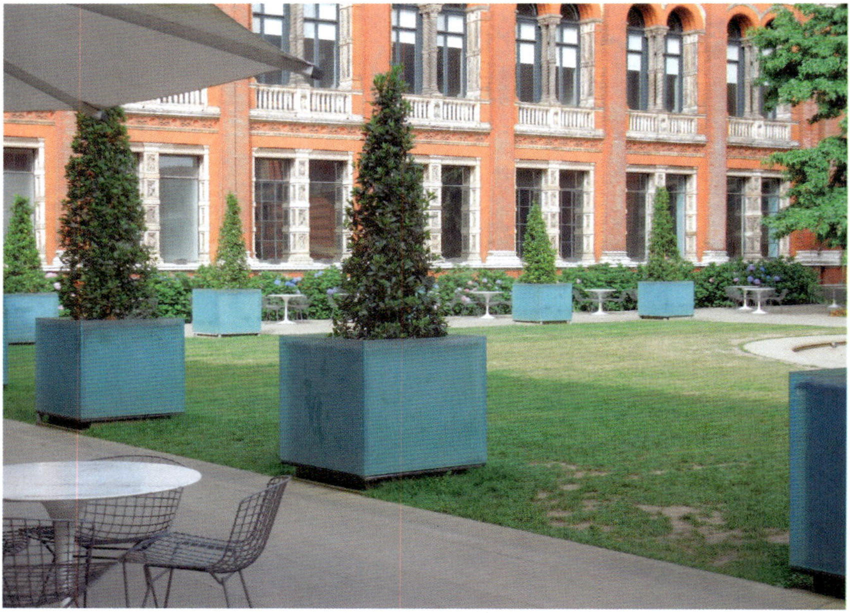

John Madejski Garden

Location: In the courtyard of the Victoria & Albert Museum
Closest Underground Station: South Kensington
Nearby Attractions: Natural History Museum, Science Museum
Hours: Daily 10:00 am to 5:45 pm, Friday to 10:00 pm
Admission: Free

Located in the courtyard of the Victoria & Albert Museum, this is a simple modern garden surrounded by ornate 19th century buildings. The Garden Café is also located here and it can become very busy around lunch time, so have a quiet cup of cappuccino early in the day as you plan your visit and before it gets too busy.

The garden was created in 2005 by landscape architect Kim Wilkie who says that his design "is based on the traditional simplicity of a garden courtyard with the drama and flexibility of a stage set." In the center is an elliptical pool which is used as a paddling pool on hot summer days. Moods can be created with jets of water, night lighting and fog. John Madejski funded the design and the garden is named after him. While the surrounding buildings are old, the garden design is modern or post-modern and it makes for a pleasing contrast.

Temporary installations add to the excitement. For example, in 2016, the courtyard was decorated with an installation called *Elytra Filament Pavilion*. Architects and engineers from the University of Stuttgart in Germany created it, "inspired by the forewing shells of flying beetles known as elytra and constructed using a novel robotic production process". The striking filaments served to provide shade to some of the outdoor areas.

The museum itself is a leading, and the world's largest, repository for the decorative arts and design. It was founded in 1852 and named after Queen Victoria and Prince Albert. Like other national museums in Britain, it is free to the public. You can also take one of their free docent's tours to further enhance your experience.

[118]

Little Venice and Regent's Canal

Location: Junction of Warwick Avenue and Harrow Road
Closest Underground Stations: Warwick Avenue (for Little Venice), Camden Town
Nearby Attractions: Regent's Park, London Zoo

LITTLE VENICE IS A CHARMING AREA AROUND BROWNING'S POOL, a picturesque basin of water where the Grand Union and Regent's Canals meet. This is an affluent neighborhood surrounded by multi-million pound homes. Moored in the canal are houseboats painted in primary colors—purples, oranges, reds, yellows and blues—each personalized with an assortment of outdoor furniture, birdhouses and plants. One houseboat is docked at the side of the lagoon and has been turned into a floating cafe (see *Waterside Cafe*).

After taking in picturesque Little Venice, you can stroll Regent's Canal along a paved walk that follows the canal all the way to Camden Lock and beyond. You'll pass beautiful mansions perched on the hillsides overlooking and reflecting in the canal waters. It is peaceful here, traveled only by the occasional walker and narrow barges that take passengers to destinations north and east of Little Venice.

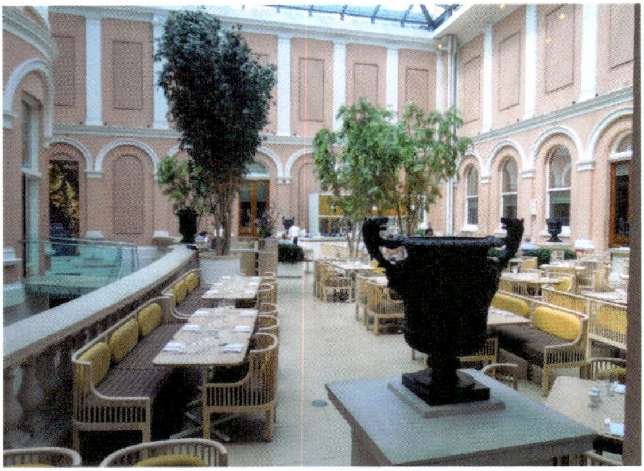

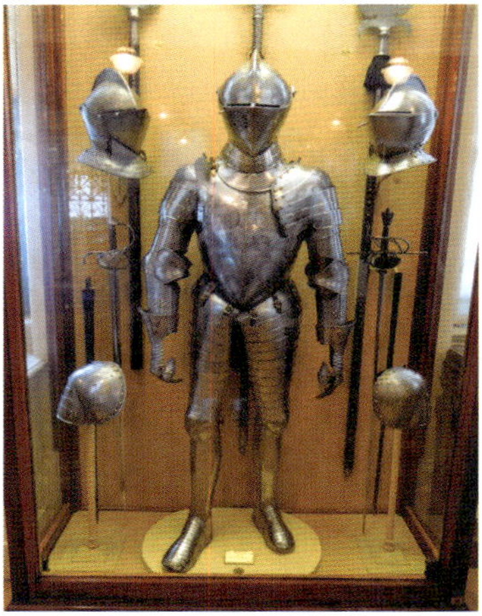

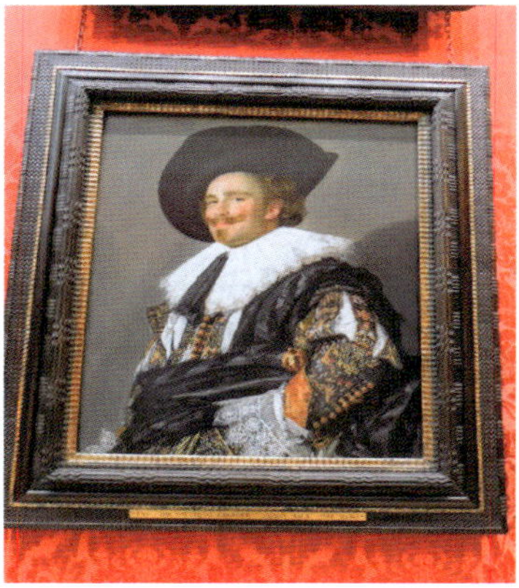

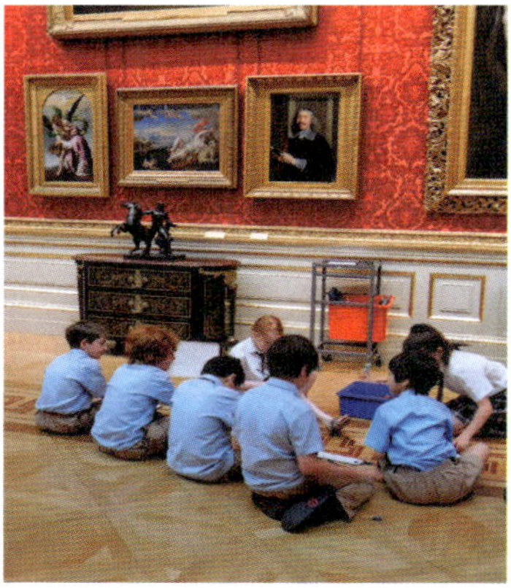

Wallace Collection

Location: Hertford House, Manchester Square
Closest Underground Stations: Bond Street, Marble Arch
Nearby Attractions: Oxford Street shopping, Hyde Park
Hours: 10am-5pm daily
Admission: Free

OFTEN OVERLOOKED BY VISITORS TO LONDON, the Wallace Collection is a private family's art collection housed inside a sumptuously furnished 18th century manor, Hertford House. It is named for Sir Richard Wallace (1818-1890), a philanthropist and art collector who came from a long line of art collectors. After his death, his widow bequeathed the house and its contents to the government. As stipulated, nothing has been added or taken away since then.

The collection includes medieval armor, French Sevres porcelain, 17th century Dutch masters, and 18th century French Rococo. Paintings by Rembrandt, Rubens, Velasquez, Titian, Gainsborough and others are on display here. Perhaps the most famous are *The Swing* by Fragonard and *The Laughing Cavalier* by Franz Hals.

Free tours are offered by art historians. And there is a pretty restaurant and cafe in the courtyard under a vaulted glass roof that serves breakfast, lunch and a reasonably priced afternoon tea.

[122]

Waterside Cafe

Location: On a boat off Warwick Crescent in Little Venice
Closest Underground Station: Warwick Avenue
Nearby Attractions: Little Venice and Regent's Canal
Hours: 9am-5pm daily

DINING AT THE WATERSIDE CAFE COMPLETES THE LITTLE VENICE EXPERIENCE. This houseboat cafe sits among other houseboats in the basin where the Grand Union and Regent's Canals meet. It's a picturesque location in an upscale neighborhood and a good spot for people-watching.

The cafe offers hearty breakfasts all day long, light meals, jacket potatoes, omelets, salads, paninis and sandwiches. If the weather is good, you can eat outside at one of several tables set up on the side of the lagoon, but even on a rainy day it's a quaint and cozy place to be.

After breakfast, join the joggers and walkers on the paved pathway along the side of the canal.

INDEX

B
Banqueting House	8
Bank of England Museum	72
Bankside Gallery	82
Battersea Park – Festival Pleasure Gardens	88
Battersea Park – Old English Garden	86
Berkeley Square	14
Blewcoat School	10
Bloomsbury Square	48
British Library	50

C
Carlyle's House	90
Charles Dickens' House	52
Chelsea Physic Garden	92
Cloisters of Westminster Abbey	12
Courtauld Institute, Art Gallery of	36

D
Design Museum	102
Dickens' House, Charles	52
Dutch Gardens in Holland Park	104

F
Faraday Museum	16
Festival Pleasure Gardens in Battersea Park	88
Fitzroy Square	54
Foundling Museum	56

G
Guildhall Art Gallery	74

H
Holland Park	104

I
Institute of Contemporary Arts	18
Italian Garden in Kensington Gardens	106

J
Japanese Gardens in Holland Park	104
John Madejski Garden in V&A Museum	116
Judd Street Open Space	58

INDEX (CONT'D)

K
Kensington Gardens' Italian Garden 106
Kensington Roof Gardens 108

L
Leighton House Museum and Art Gallery 110
Lincoln's Inn and Lincoln's Inn Fields 66
Little Venice 118
London Transport Museum 38

M
Margravine Cemetery 112
Mount Street Gardens 20

N
National Portrait Gallery 30

O
Old Burial Ground, Royal Hospital of Chelsea 96
Old English Garden in Battersea Park 86

P
Photographers' Gallery 32
Physic Garden, Chelsea 92
Pollock's Toy Museum 60

Q
Queen's Chapel of the Savoy 40

R
Regent's Canal 118
Roof Gardens, Kensington 108
Roper's Garden 94
Royal Hospital of Chelsea, Old Burial Ground 96
Russell Square 62

S
Saatchi Gallery 98
Savoy Chapel 40
Sir John Soane's Museum 70
Soane, Sir John 70
Somerset House 36
Southwark Cathedral's Milllenium Courtyard 84
Spencer House 26
Spreads Cafe & Deli 28
St. Andrew Holborn Church 68

INDEX (CONT'D)

St. James Church	22
St. James Square	24
St. Luke Parish Church's Gardens	100
St. Martin-in-the-Fields	34
St. Mary Abbots Schoolyard and Alleyway	114
St. Mary-le-Strand	42
St. Michael's Cornhill's Garden	76
St. Pancras Parish Church	64
St. Paul's Cathedral's Courtyards	78
St. Paul's Church	44
St. Stephen Walbrook	80

V

Victoria & Albert Museum, John Madejski Garden	116
Victoria Embankment Gardens	46

W

Wallace Collection	120
Waterside Cafe	122
Westminster Abbey's Cloisters	12

Index	125

About the Author

Elizabeth von Pier is a retired banker who travels the world. In her retirement, she finally has time to travel extensively and pursue her interests in writing, photography and publishing. Her articles have been published in the Los Angeles Times, Go Nomad, Travel Thru History, Hackwriters and various online magazines. When she's home, Ms. von Pier lives in Hingham, Massachusetts, a quaint seaside community south of Boston. This is her first book.

NOTES

NOTES

NOTES

Printed in Great Britain
by Amazon